STRENGTH AND TENDERNESS

HYMNS, SONGS, POEMS

DOUG CONSTABLE

Copyright © Doug Constable 2021.
All rights reserved.

Print ISBN 978-1-8384289-6-9

The right of Doug Constable to be identified as the author of this work has been asserted by him in accordance with the Copyright Designs and Patents Act 1988

No part of this publication may be reproduced, stored in a retrieval system, or transmitted in any form or by any means without the prior permission in writing of the publisher. Nor be otherwise circulated in any form or binding or cover other than that in which it is published and without a similar condition being imposed on the subsequent purchaser.

The hymns, words, and musical settings of Doug Constable may be reprinted or reproduced by members of the Church Copyright Licence International service and/or the ONE LICENSE service, provided the items copied are included on their royalty reports.

Published by
Llyfrau Cambria Books, Wales, United Kingdom.
Cambria Books is a division of
Cambria Publishing.
Discover our other books at: www.cambriabooks.co.uk

REVIEWS

"This is an exciting collection that will not only enrich the musical life of a worshipping community but also their theological understanding... The inclusion of the stories behind the pieces is refreshing – restoring the connection between hymnody and the ordinary lives of those seeking a Christian way in a complex world."
Rev June Boyce-Tillman, MBE, Professor Emerita of Applied Music, Winchester University.

"When I first met Doug in the 1970's I was really inspired by his energy and his ability to engage through his music in such an open and honest way. In this mighty collection it is clear that he loves music and loves words, but perhaps most of all, he loves people. He is a wonderful, natural communicator whose work shines with warmth and integrity and he has the ability to say something very profound often through disarmingly simple means, which is a great gift."
Bob Chilcott, Composer, Principal Guest Conductor BBC Singers

"I have been moved and challenged by Doug's words and music for the past five decades. Singing his songs with others has drawn us together, inspired by his loving, believing take on life. They are unique and this collection is a treasure store."
Elizabeth Hume, Teacher

"Within this extraordinary collection of hymns, of words and ... wonderfully original musical arrangements, chord progressions and melodies, you will find yourself reading, then singing, truly beautiful, insightful and prophetic words - hymns that will, perhaps, challenge your whole experience of congregational expression and proclamation."
Adrian Snell, Composer, Recording Artist, Music Therapist

"The hymns and poems in this book ... are strong, line by line, in rhythm and form, and tender in their recognition of human weakness and their faith... Many are admirably suited to public worship, and would make fine additions to any hymnal."
J.Richard Watson, Professor Emeritus of English Literature, Durham University, author of The English Hymn (Oxford 1999

"Doug Constable's hymn-writing has come out of the encounter between an unusually fresh imagination and a series of very specific pastoral contexts; and this means that it is exploratory, genuinely celebratory, challenging, and mercifully free of cliché - both traditional and contemporary cliché. These are humane, candid compositions, and they will be a real gift to all who are looking for words and music that are neither frozen in inherited attitudes nor labouring for an emotional quick fix. I hope they will be welcomed, used and loved."
Rowan Williams, Archbishop Emeritus, Honorary President of The Hymn Society of Great Britain and Ireland).

DEDICATION

To Valerie Faith, whose full faith steadies my compass,
and to all those who over the years have encouraged me to 'stick at it'.

ACKNOWLEDGEMENTS

Family of the late Alice Evans for 'Ym Methlem datguddiwyd'
Friends of York Minster for 'O Lord Jesus Christ
Michael Cottam for the music setting LLANGADOG
Stainer & Bell for 'Warm God of seeds' and 'Where is he? the wise men asking'

PERMISSIONS SOUGHT

Siân Rhiannon for 'Daw llafn o haul'
OUP for 'Lord of all hopefulness'

TABLE OF CONTENTS

Words and music by DC
Words only by DC
MUSIC ONLY BY DC
Poem by DC

1   All my strength and tenderness
2   Alive to God in Jesus Christ
3   **And did that Love in times gone by**
4   **Appeal to God, my sisters and my brothers**
5   **As we share this life between us**
6   Be it done to me according to Thy word
     'A Ballad of Bethle...hum'
7   Before our minds conceived the source of life
8   BLESS TO ME, O GOD (Prayer at Dressing)
9   BREATHE ON ME, O BREATH OF GOD
10   **Called to worship by Your Spirit**
     Annunciation
11   Child of our time
12   Christ calls us salt
     Art-Singer
13   CHRIST IS THE LORD OF THE SMALLEST ATOM
14   **Christ our Shepherd, all souls hauling**
15   Come, Flame and Fire of Divine Love
16   **Come, let me grow to know my Father's business**
     Changing the Agenda: An Easter Ditty
17   Come, make way for the music
     Comforter
18   Companion me, and eat my bread
     Commission
19   DAW LLAFN O HAUL (A ray of sunshine)
20   **Dear God, I pray you, save**
21   **Dear Source of joy, whence love is spawned**
     Crucifixion Evening
22   Despised, rejected servant
23   **Do not let your hearts be troubled**
24   DOWN WENT MARY
25   From far away I hear you calling me
26   FROM GLORY TO GLORY ADVANCING
27   **God's boundless love, the universe enfolding**
28   **God, in-breathing Holy Scripture**
29   God, whose nature is to share
30   God, you look within the heart

31 He comes, unknown, to be baptized
32 Here we stand, we Christian people
    Fresh Springs
33 I am among you as one in danger
34 I cannot look on Thee, to Love I said
35 Image and likeness of God is our union
36 **In the Church of the Unlikely**
37 In this dark world unending light
    Gospel Procession
38 Into a stream of passing days
39 I took the work you offered
40 It's time once more to turn to the door
41 Jesus Christ was handed over
42 **Jesus, light of heaven**
    Holy Week 1995
43 Jesus, our sacrifice
    In Memoriam Alan Kurdi (3)
44 Jesus says, Here am I (The Body Song)
45 **'Jesus' they named you**
46 Judge of all peoples
47 Let there be peace on the earth
48 Let this mind be in me
    Lord, with each breath I take
49 Life, life, eternal life!
50 Looking at you
51 Looking for you, always, everywhere
52 LORD OF ALL HOPEFULNESS
    Love's Coming
53 **Mary, weep not, weep no longer**
54 Most Holy Jesus (1) & Lord of life's journey (2)
55 Mysterious Lord of every dream
56 No one remembers my mother, my father
57 O LORD JESUS CHRIST (A Priest's Prayer)
58 O Blessed Fire within, beyond
59 O GOD OF BETHEL, BY WHOSE HAND
60 O Hidden Source of Love
61 O LORD, WE LONG TO SEE YOUR FACE
62 O my people, sisters, brothers
    Mercredi des Cendres
63 **O Thou beyond all culture, creed, and caste**
64 O Thou the Breath, the Light of all
65 **O Thou, who came to serve**
66 One dark night
    On fearing and not fearing
67 Out of the ground we hear the cry

68	PRAISE MY SOUL THE KING OF HEAVEN
69	PRAY THAT JERUSALEM MAY HAVE
	Salem Stones: a homily
70	Revitalise our spirits, Lord
71	***Soul of creation, soul of life***
72	Send us out in the power of thy Spirit
73	Shall the wolf live with the lamb?
74	Sovereign of each unfolding hour
75	***Star-guided pilgrims***
76	Stations of the Cross
	Sing out, my soul
77	Summoned by your call
78	TAKE UP THY CROSS, THE SAVIOUR SAID
79	TEACH ME, MY GOD AND KING
	Socially-distanced Christmas
80	The Most High made a garden
81	The source of life, at first
	St Dwynwen's Day
82	There is a gift we cannot grasp
	Sunday morning a while ago
83	***There is a love more perfect***
84	There's laughter in the loins of those
85	THY KINGDOM COME, O GOD
86	This body, Lord, is mine and yours
	The Deanery House, Southampton
87	This night the grace of God has conquered
88	THROUGH THE NIGHT OF DOUBT AND SORROW
89	To signify your presence
90	VICTIM DIVINE, THY GRACE WE CLAIM
	The Long Watch on Holocaust Memorial Day
91	Warm God of seeds
92	We see you, Lord, through mercy's lens
93	***When in the wastes of wild regret***
94	What kind of human
95	When terror strikes
	Upstairs -Downstairs
96	WHERE IS HE? THE WISE MEN ASKING
97	Whoever you are
98	With fervent thanksgiving, with love in my heart
99	Within the commonwealth of God
	When you surveyed, with no note lost
100	YM METHLEM DATGUDDIWYD Y GAIR
101	You break the bar, the yoke, the rod

INTRODUCTION

Why this book?

For over fifty years I have composed the words and music to many hymns, songs, anthems, and poems. I am not adept at using the technology that could have made them available before now, and they have spent most of their time quietly sleeping in lever arch files on shelves in our home; so I only rarely play or sing any of them. Some of those hymns and songs are collected into this book, and they can now take their proper place at the keyboard, ready to be played and sung and shared with other people.

When I recently had occasion to review much of my shelved collection, I found – in John Wesley's disarming phrase – *my heart strangely warmed*. I knew many folks had been moved by some of these hymns, so that made another reason for publishing; if others came to know some of these pieces, their hearts might be gladdened as well.

How it is laid out

Following the pattern in one of my favourite collections, *100 Hymns for Today*, published in 1969 by Hymns Ancient and Modern Limited, I have laid out these pieces without regard to themes or chronology. With a few exceptions, the order is determined by alphabetical sequence. To enable consistent pagination while avoiding blank pages, at irregular intervals poems are interspersed with the hymns.

While any or all of the pieces in this collection can be photocopied for use in worship or other settings, the volume as a whole, being in the nature of an archive, is not set out as a hymnal ready for use in church; there are, for example, no author, biblical, or metrical indexes. A note on its provenance or significance accompanies nearly every piece. Where Bible references are given, looking up those references should prove helpful.

The hymns are in a variety of styles and genres, including several that would more usually be called songs, and a few that could pass as hymn-anthems. If used in shared worship, some could be readily sung by congregations, some would certainly need learning in advance, and a few might be best offered on behalf of, rather than by, a congregation.

Background

I trust the impulse to compose music and words together needs no justification, but some may wonder whether there's much call for putting different words or music to well-loved tunes or words. Having myself been prejudiced for years against people 'mucking about' with words and music that evidently belonged together and that many of us love, I had 'an epiphany moment' in 1972, during the first and only time I heard a new setting of *When I survey the wondrous cross*, sung live. It was part of a staged revue about the Passion of Jesus, and, because the performers weren't singing it to ROCKINGHAM, I bridled at the sound of the first two verses. But by the fifth and last I was swooning with admiration for the way words, music, and performance had drawn me into the hymn's matter: I was being faced close up by my crucified Lord in a way I'd not experienced since, as a choirboy more than twenty years previously, I had sung in Edward Bairstow's *Lamentations*. This music to *When I survey* lent fresh, intense colouring to Isaac Watts' words, and a piece that till then I had sung solely as a piece of devotional recitation suddenly became a dramatic encounter, for the singers as well as many of us in the audience.

The composer, producer of this 'Gospel Revue', and its piano accompanist was Philip Humphreys (1936-2017), senior chaplain at Lee Abbey in Devon, and the cast were fellow members of the Community. Through this and other revues Philip and company together preached with arresting, unforgettable imagery. I learned later that Philip's substantial body of work was unpublished; his sole concern was proclamation and encounter in the here-and-now. His musical settings – many to hugely popular hymns that, words and music together, I'd hitherto taken to be pillars of a fixed spiritual universe – functioned as instruments for freshly engaging our minds-in-our-hearts with the reality of Holy Presence always and everywhere.

Inspired and encouraged by them all, when I became a member of the Community, I began to develop my own musical-dramatic impulses and understandings. Twenty-five years later, after joining the Hymn Society of Great Britain and Ireland, I realized that most of the hymns I had been composing till then were in styles not considered suitable for congregational singing; quite a few were written to be performed on stage, and this had spilled over into the way I thought about singing generally in church.

Two examples in this book illustrate the point.

I wrote *Be it done to me according to Thy word* for a dozen or so mostly elderly members of our Mothers' Union to present - meaning, perform - during a Eucharist for Mothering Sunday. When I first introduced it to them, they were sure they could never manage to sing it; but they buckled down, and in the event (sic) their rendition was spirited and joyful, and I believe the congregation was delighted and helped by hearing them. It would be gratifying to know of any congregations who might follow their example with any of the hymns or musical settings in this book.

In a dramatic presentation at Lee Abbey about St Mark's Gospel, my setting of *From glory to glory advancing* was composed to give expression to the imagined emotions of the thousands who were miraculously fed from five loaves and two fishes. Fans of any Cup Final team leading by three goals to nil with ten minutes left to play might readily relate to this tune.

Influences

As a writer, composer, and preacher, I am keenly aware that very many influences bear on us all. Many hymns live deep within me; I met the first few of this brief list as a choirboy in Dorking.

Pre-eminent is *O thou who camest from above* by Charles and Samuel Sebsatian Wesley, closely followed by *At the name of Jesus*, sung to KINGS WESTON, the stirring setting by R.Vaughan Williams. I find the second line of James Turle's music to F.W.Faber's *My God, how wonderful thou art* difficult to sing, but this hymn of adoration sings itself in my heart. In Junior School, *God is love, his the care* became inscribed into my spiritual DNA, while from student years in East London, both *O God of earth and altar* and *Judge eternal, clothed in splendour* helped cement my emerging political convictions. From '100 Hymns for Today', I treasure Timothy Rees' *O crucified Redeemer*, and I am continually inspired by Sydney Carter's *Every star shall sing a carol*. Today, I am grateful to be acquainted with many contemporary hymns and some of their writers; some, if I live long enough, will no doubt appear in a future list of those that have influenced me most.

So nearly seventy years after I finished being a choirboy, the experience of being under the direction of Dr William Cole (1909-97) still impacts on me. Through the 1960s the 20th Century Church Light Music Group and Stainer & Bell's 'Faith, Folk and Clarity' all helped lighten my natural ponderousness. Judith Piepe (1920-2003) (who helped Paul Simon get launched) pushed me to venture my first songs. A school friend, Charles Harvey (1940-2010), got me to write music for an (unperformed) musical, a version of 'The Rake's Progress'. In addition to Philip Humphreys, some of the other priests who encouraged me to write were Robin

Morrell (1929-2010), Peter Coleman (1928-2001), and Stephen Verney (1919-2009). Nicola Slee, poet and practical theologian, was a valued companion as I tried to 'up' my hymn-writing efforts; as was June Boyce-Tillman, priest, teacher of applied music, and composer. June helped me recover momentum after I had 'dried up' at one stage, strongly urging me to come to King Alfred's College (now the University of Winchester), where, with Elizabeth Stuart, she facilitated my composing many hymns while researching my hymn-writing process. During that time, some of my work was constructively criticised by poet and URC minister, Alan Gaunt; late in my life, Alan's stringent observations have helpfully sharpened my self-critical faculties. To all of these, with others too many to name, I am deeply grateful.

As I review these, some of my strongest influences, a further name stands out: Geoffrey Paul (1921-83). A warm pastor blessed with huge vision and intellect, Geoffrey encouraged his charges, me among them, in the words of William Carey (1761-1834) to 'attempt great things for God and expect great things from God'. He was himself a passionate worker for Christianly-human (not just separately Christian) unity. Once, when he was Warden of Lee Abbey, during rehearsals for a musical production I was in process of writing, some members of the community not taking part in the production mounted, on theological grounds, an organised public attack on part of the work. It was a delicate, almost make-or-break moment for the production and for me as an artist: was my work for the greater glory of God and furthering of the common good? or an ambitious piece of self-indulgence, 'a vain thing'? Geoffrey respectfully engaged with the critics, drew their sting, and enabled us all (I hope this is true) to become more united and eager to press forward with our shared project.

Appreciations

My wife, Valerie, and our children, Jessica, Benjamin, and Hannah have kept up waves of encouragement over the decades, and I am overwhelmed by their love. Val has contributed an image to this book, one of her 'Eight Paintings of the Passion' of 1994, which Ben has designed into its cover; an outer garment for the body within.

In the 1990s I attended some classes in Musical Theory taught by prolific composer, John Webber, now living in the U.S.A. John directed my attention to 'voice leading', an indispensable tool for composers of hymn-settings. We have stayed in touch, and I am grateful for his helping me lay out some of the music in this collection.

Until I first acquired Sibelius software, most of my music was only roughly noted, sometimes almost illegibly. I am grateful to everyone who helped me gain enough facility with computers not only to be able to gather my work into some sort of order, but to edit, and in some cases properly 'compose', some of the music for the first time.

I had been making heavy weather of getting this collection into publishable form, and it was a relief when, late in the day, I learned that a close neighbour, Chris Jones, is the owner of Cambria Publishing. I am fortunate to have been able to draw on Chris' 'Authors' Services' in the critical final stages before printing, and I thank him most warmly.

Envoi

In, and beyond my immediate helpers, I am in debt – as are we all – to the Creator Spirit who gifts us the resources and means to respond to the generosity that we sometimes recognise as 'Original Blessing'. It is a privilege to be able to work, to make pieces. I delight in knowing and feeling both that our personal offerings – our 'little drop of water and little grain of sand' (to quote from my Infants' School hymn-book) help to 'make the mighty ocean and the beauteous land', and that each of us can contribute to the Church's offering of divine worship in the voice of all Creation. As best I can express it, that's where these hymns come from. I hope they help you voice some of your own offerings of *wonder, love and praise*.

Doug Constable
Llandeilo Summer 2021

1

TEILO MAGNIFICAT 7777
Two-part round

Words and music
Doug Constable
© 2005

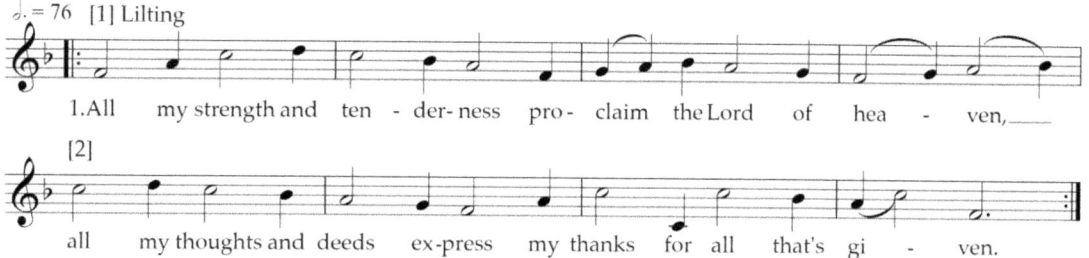

All my strength and tenderness
proclaim the Lord of heaven;
all my thought and deeds express
my thanks for all that's given.

Love has sprung to life in me,
has made me great, though lowly;
far and near sing "Blessed is she
by God, whose name is holy."

God exalts the humble, poor,
and grace supplies the needy;
truth undoes the proud and, more,
deprives the rich and greedy.

This fulfilment God inspired
before our hope conceived it;
ages long this gift desired,
and faith has now achieved it.

Glory to the living Lord:
All-Love, Beloved, and Loving.
Heaven and earth in one accord
this joyful truth is proving.

*Invited to speak to the Mothers' Union of Llandeilo Fawr,
I composed this song to be a two-part canon for them.
It would make an excellent piece for dancing to,
perhaps accompanied just by flute/recorder and tambour.*

2

MUKTIBAR CM

Words and Music
Doug Constable
© 2003

♩ = 100

1. A-live to God in Jesus Christ: we count our-selves as so; then, since the world is sick with lust, we rage at ev-'ry woe.
2. We rage in grief for laugh-ter's ghost when child-ren cease to play; when Jews' and Gent-iles' young are lost to hat-red's dead-ly sway.
3. We rage in pain for love de-ranged when each the oth-er slays, when hon-our needs must be a-venged, and blood for more blood bays.
4. We rage in shame for friends be-trayed to jeal-ous-y and fear, who, choice-less, bear re-ject-ion's load, while help is no-where near.

5. We rage in guilt for our a-buse of peo-ple we dis-dain: those we op-press ex-pose in us our screams of hid-den pain.
6. You see, You hear, You laugh, You play, while love is cru-ci-fied: so does God care when peo-ple cry, and ev-'ry hope has died?
7. Yet some can see a well near by, find wat-er-life with-in. Christ, grant us all this bless-ing too; let sib-ling peace be-gin.

Alive to God in Jesus Christ:
we count ourselves as so;
then since the world is sick with lust,
we rage at every woe.

We rage in grief for laughter's ghost
when children cease to play:
when Jews' and Gentiles' young are lost
to hatred's deadly sway.

We rage in pain for love deranged
when each the other slays,
when honour needs must be avenged,
and blood for more blood bays.

We rage in shame for friends betrayed
to jealousy and fear,
who, choiceless, bear rejection's load,
while help is nowhere near.

We rage in guilt for our abuse
of people we disdain;
whom we oppress expose in us
our screams of hidden pain.

You see, You hear, You laugh and play,
while love is crucified:
so does God care when people cry,
and every hope has died?

Yet some can see a well nearby,
find water-life within.
Christ, grant us all this blessing too;
let sibling-peace begin.

Genesis 21.8-21

The background to this hymn is in the story, after the birth of Isaac, of Abraham and Sarah rejecting Hagar, her maid, and Ishmael, Hagar's son by Abraham. The hymn rages with Hagar against the cruelty and injustice inflicted on her and Ishmael. Lest it become an excuse for projecting onto others, in verse 5 we acknowledge our own collusion with the abuses we deplore. In verse 6 "You see" is the name Hagar gives to God, who sees her afflicted state; and "You hear" is the meaning of Ishmael: it is Hagar's gratitude for being promised a future on earth.

Mukti Barton alerted me to the force of Hagar's rage, and for the need for Christians to be in solidarity with her.

3

And did that Love, in times gone by,
work within all our hopes and dreams?
And did that Touch, that Heart, that Voice
make holy all life's common themes?
And was the Wonder, Power, and Joy,
alive in us, making us new?
And was the heaven of grace builded here
where daily I go on with you?

Here is my strength pledged for your peace,
here my respect, my truth, my good,
here all my tenderness, my tears,
my friendship, and my heart's best food.
I will not cease to praise the light,
nor shall my heart yield up its gains,
till we have built our house of love,
and Love for ever in us reigns.

Words: © Doug Constable 1999/2021
(after William Blake (1757-1827)
Music: Charles.Hubert.Parry (1848-1918)

I was called at short notice to conduct a wedding in a neighbouring parish. At the rehearsal I learned that the couple had chosen JERUSALEM to be one of their hymns, a choice I'd not previously encountered (though I now know it's a popular choice). It prompted me to compose an alternative …

4

Appeal to God, my sisters and my brothers,
to Christ the Lord, made judge of all the earth;
appeal beyond the pride of blood and nation
to One who works all good, brings love to birth.
For Christ is risen, Christ once dead and buried!
Love triumphs over all that makes for fear
and life lifts high each soul in new beginning,
sends blessings everywhere both far and near.

Appeal to God, my brothers and my sisters,
to Christ the Lord, whom cosmic powers obey;
appeal beyond the clamour of self-interest,
to One who cares for all, shows life's true way.
For Christ has conquered, Christ once thought defeated!
Compassion covers sins of every kind,
and faith empowers each soul for new beginnings;
grounds all in hope, creates love's ties that bind.

Words: © 1997 Doug Constable
Music: DERRY AIR Trad.Irish
Metre: 11 10 11 10

1 Peter 3.22
Anticipating the celebration of Christ's Ascension, this hymn celebrates a remarkable fact of history: that a small, first-century sect within the Roman Empire proclaimed that 'their' God had gone into heaven…with angels, authorities and powers made subject to him. And they set this proclamation within the rite of baptism: new members were baptised, not merely into the culture of their local congregation and tribe, but into the universal Church, whose business, under God, was nothing less than the salvation of humankind within the universe.
DERRY AIR was chosen as the melody for this hymn as soon as the first words presented themselves.

5

As we share this life between us,
feeding, clothing, honouring all,
caring to restore the meanest,
we are honouring heaven's call.
Grace through one shows love embodied,
love that none but grace has known;
grace, the song of God encoded,
gives, receives love's life, love's own.

Holy Spirit, seed, solution,
source inbreathing fruitful lives,
gathering into heaven's ocean
earth's beloved, freedom's slaves:
touch our eyes, our hearts, our voices,
kindle praise, and faith, and sight;
in the way, truth, life rejoicing,
all in grace of love unite.

Words: © 1997 Doug Constable
Music: PLEADING SAVIOUR
Plymouth (USA) Collection 1855
Metre: 8787 D

2 Corinthians 13.14
These words aim at expounding the prayer known as 'The Grace', which is thought particularly suitable for celebrating the Holy Trinity. Unlike Reginald Heber's great hymn 'Holy, Holy, Holy Lord God Almighty', where God is imaged in state, like a feudal lord receiving his vassals' pledges of loyal service, in 'The Grace' God goes forth as "grace", "love", "fellowship", each noun representing God building and restoring the community of Creation.

6

THOMAS' MAGNIFICAT 11 11 11 11 12 12 12 12

Words and Music:
Doug Constable
© 1978

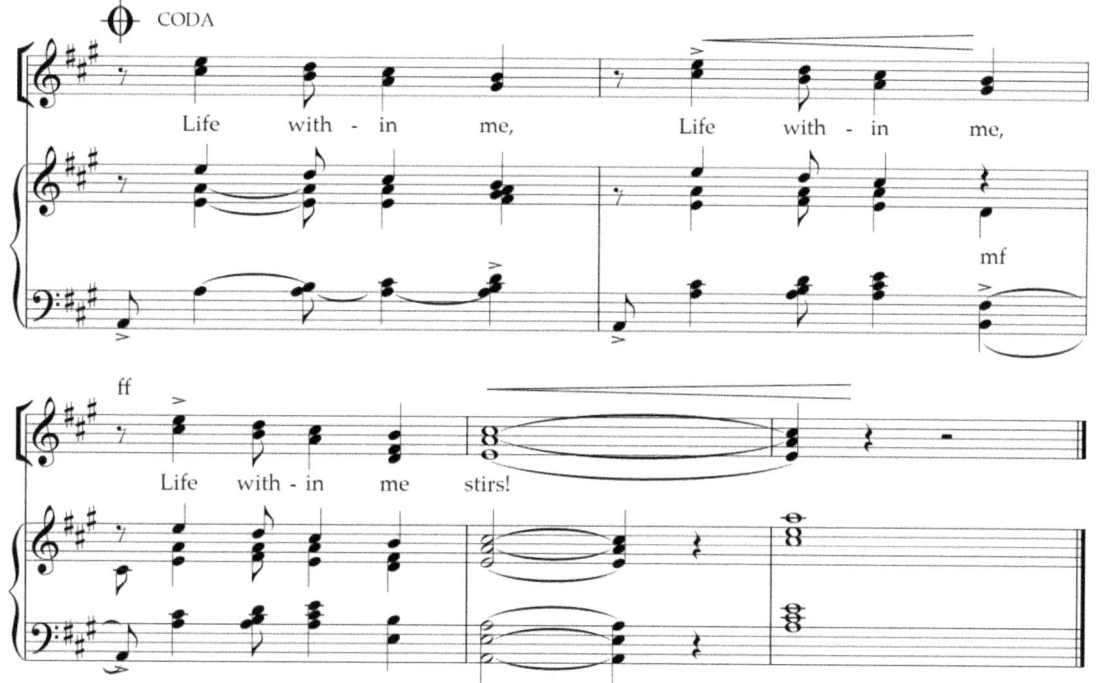

Refrain
Be it done to me according to Your word.
May my destiny be all You have prepared.
Let my future fulfil what You've prepared.
Now my heart awakes: life within me stirs!

Bearer of Love to me, You bring my Christ to me,
and lodge Love's mystery in my unworthy soul.
Sharer of blood with me, You show my Lord to me,
and lead all history to God-in-me-made-whole. So…
Refrain

He is the Lord of power, of every place and hour;
He rules both rich and poor, and helps the people in need;
Each age He cares the same for those who fear His name;
He takes away their shame, and sets them each one free. So… **Refrain**

I give You glory, Lord, for all Your love outpoured,
for all my life restored by Your almighty Love.
To Father, Saviour-Son, and Holy Spirit, One,
may praise on praise be sung in earth and heaven above. So… **Refrain**

Luke 1.46-55
In St Thomas' Derby at the Parish Eucharist on Mothering Sunday it had been the custom for our Branch of the Mothers' Union to sing *Shall we not love thee, Mother dear?* To offer them an alternative, I wrote this versification of Mary's Song. Cautious at first, Branch members took to it willingly and presented it with verve and joy.

'A Ballad of Bethle...hum'
Homily for St John's Maesteilo

I tell the tale of Dai and Mair,
   who live not far from here;
they keep their sheep, sing in the choir,
   greet every day with cheer.

An angel called on them one day,
   a clipboard in her hand:
"Please take parts in our Christmas play;
   it's great, but not too grand."

"Shall I be Joe?" asked Dai, all keen.
   Said Mair, "Be Mary, I?"
"Sort of", the angel said: "I mean,
   we'll need you by and by."

She led them from the bryn, along
   the afon in the cwm,
and, as she went, taught them a song
   she wanted them to hum.

Said Dai to Mair, and Mair to Dai,
   and they did both agree,
"We're extras in this play. But why
   choose you? And why choose me?"

At length they came to Bethlehem,
   where there was quite a throng
all standing round, waiting, like them,
   to hum the simple song.

"Action!" the angel called at last;
   they thought, "Now here we go".
"Not you," said she: "the creatures first.
   Cocks: crow! and cattle: low!"

There in the stable, ass ee-awed,
   hens clucked, and pony neighed;
the baby woke, cried loud; the Lord
   mewled while the donkey brayed.

Mair looked at Dai, and Dai at Mair,
   wonder was in their eyes,
for they were hearing a holy choir;
   it made them humble, wise.

Then someone whispered, "Glory be";
   the word went round, "Now hum";
the extras all pressed forward to see;
   they heard, "You're all well come."

"Makes all the difference," they agreed
   "that, in the manger crude,
the baby – one of us indeed! –
   is – dare we say it? – GOD."

Now that they've gone back to their sheep,
   and pipe up in the choir –
he as Bryn Terfel, she Bo-peep –
   Dai Joseff, Mary Mair,

they stride the bryn, and sing of love
   that meets them where they are
and lifts them to the heights above,
   where every saint's a star.

My tale is done of Mair and Dai
   (they're really you and me).
When angels call you, say "Aye aye",
   then hum your 'Glory be'.

                Christmas 2015

7

Before our minds conceived the force of life expanding,
before our thoughts disclosed the maze of time abounding,
before our words proclaimed a god all works transcending,
    Love gave birth.

Before our sense awoke to joy of life evolving,
before our muse discerned great mystery unfolding,
before our hearts embraced truth's mystery unclosing,
    Love stood forth.

Before the dream declined of heaven in our lifetime,
before our eyes grew dim along this mortal lifeline,
before our world expired, all memory gone to silence,
    Love blessed death.

And still our Love's alive beyond what's past our knowing;
indeed, our Love's engaged with making whole and growing;
and, yes, our Love's committed to the goal of being.
    We draw breath.

Come, praise this Love who bears the force of life expanding,
confess this Love embodied through all time abounding,
and serve this Love who dies and lives, all death transcending:
    Christ on earth!

This was written in Southampton for a Eucharist whose theme, under the guidance of Chris Clarke (1946-2018), was 'Creation Spirituality'. Its inspiration comes from Julian of Norwich: *I saw for certain…that before ever he made us, God loved us; and that his love has never slackened, nor ever shall…. Our beginning was when we were made, but the love in which he made us never had a beginning. In it we have our beginning.*
In verse 1 'god' is un-capitalized because conceived by humans (whereas G*d is beyond human conceiving).

THAGASTE 13 13 13 3

Words and Music
Doug Constable © 1996

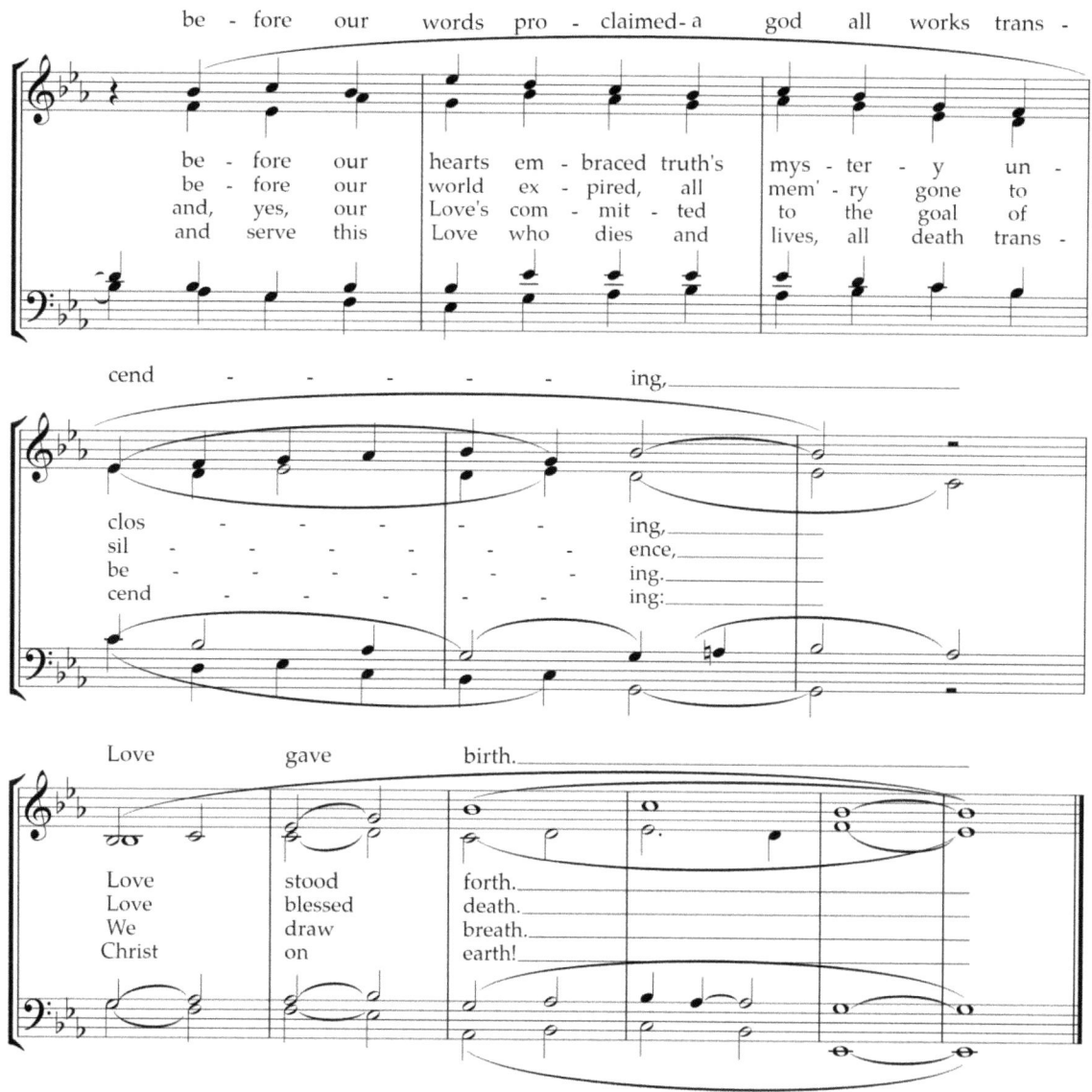

8
Carmina Gadelica 1900

Doug Constable
© 1995

This lovely *Prayer at Dressing* could 'work' for anyone uncomfortable with 'churchy' ways of praying.

9

Edwin Hatch 1835-89 — Doug Constable
RATTAN SM ♩ = 104 Molto Legato
© 1998

1. Breathe on me, O Breath of God,
Fill me with life, with life anew,
That I may love what thou dost love,
And do what thou would'st do,
And do what thou would'st do.

2.3.4. Breathe on me, O Breath of God,
until my heart is pure,
until with thee I will one will,
to do and to endure,
to do and to endure.

(verse 3) till I am wholly thine;
until this earthly part of me
glows with thy fire divine,
glows with thy fire divine.

(verse 4) so shall I never die,
but live with thee the perfect life
of thine eternity,
of thine eternity.

John 20.22
A dear friend with who had asthma asked me to set these beloved words. It is hoped that RATTAN will help worshippers practice breathing, both when singing and in everyday life.

Called to worship by Your Spirit,
drawn with others to Your love,
seeking fellowship, we dare it –
hands reach out, Your grace to prove.
In Your sanctuary we gather
life's rich river flowing through,
singing, "Jesus, Spirit, Father,
love's fresh springs are all in You."

Springing from the depths of Godhead,
winding, finding love's own way,
Living Water from the Well-head,
Fount of Joy, in whom we pray:
bless us in this ancient valley,
sift each soul, make all things new;
cleanse, and turn us to You daily;
our fresh springs are all in You.

Tywi's saints, dear God, with Dewi,
stand before You, hearts on fire:
Cynwyl joins with Porthmon Caio,
Sawyl, Sadwrn, Santes Mair,
Cwrdaf, Dingat, Pantycelyn
always still the song renew;
Egwad, Cadog, Teilo, Cathen:
their fresh springs are all in You.

One with all the saints, we praise You,
each with voice unique, and tongue;
churches, chapels, all upraise You,
glorying in the Lamb's high song.
As we pass into the future,
grant us faith, our hope renew;
may we know, with every creature,
heaven's fresh springs are all in You.

Psalm 87.7 Coverdale 1535 "The singers also and the trumpeters shall he rehearse: All my fresh springs shall be in thee."
In October 2011, as part of a pan-U.K. celebration of the seventy-fifth birthday of The Hymn Society of Great Britain and Ireland, a bi-lingual interdenominational festival 'Cenwch Clod Ddyffryn Tywi Valley Sing Praise' was held at Capel Salem in Llandeilo Fawr. Giving expression to some of the Towy Valley's spiritual history as well as its topography, this hymn was written for that festival, to music by Revd Michael Cottam, who also conducted the singing and the instrumentalists. The text, launched essentially as an additional hymn for the occasion, was translated into Welsh by the distinguished hymn-writer, Siôn Aled Owen.

ANNUNCIATION

Some days or weeks after I first agreed,
I sat down, dedicated to the task
of knowing what was asked of me.
In my head the accustomed sandbag,
my senses inert as usual. Doggedly
I read the text, over and over; thought a bit;
then framed some inferences that seemed
but pedantry. No joy in this. But, waiting,
dull, I learned Your musefulness. A
fountain yawn, then others, cavernous;
bugles pricked in tautening limbs; my
charging pulse would not be stilled.

Is it always Your way, to volcano the earth
when You arouse a mind to love?

6.1.1999

11

Child of our time, child of our longing,
love of our hearts, lost in our dreaming:
we are in labour, joy in our sorrow,
helpless, we wait for You to come.

Child of our blood, child of our pleading,
all of our good, all of our needing:
we are in turmoil, wills in confusion,
cursing and blessing till You come.

Child of our birth, child of our dying,
fruit of the earth, breath of our sighing:
we have grown weary, faith with excuses,
fainting, we trust that You will come.

Starting again, starting the morning,
loved into life fresh from the dayspring,
we are like children, dreams in our laughter,
years are made young by You who come.

Child, and our Lord, child of the heavens,
hope of the world, peace, and our wholeness:
we are your family, sisters and brothers,
all of one blood in You who come.

God in our flesh, God in our failing,
Light in our lives, Star in our striving:
sing we your praises – thanks in all duty -
worship you now that You are come.

In 1975 the then Archbishops of Canterbury and York published a *Call to the Nation*. This hymn was written for participants at a conference held at Lee Abbey in November 1975 to consider this *Call*.
Although the hymn can be sung at any time of the year, it is perhaps most suitable for Christmas and Epiphany.

BLANCHCOGGAN 9 9 10 8

♩. = 64 Smooth, lilting, whole-line phrases

UNISON

1. Child of our time, child of our longing,
   love of our hearts, lost in our dreaming:
   we are in labour, joy in our sorrow;
   helpless, we wait for you to come.

2. Child of our blood, child of our pleading,
   all of our good, all of our needing:
   we are in turmoil, wills in confusion,
   cursing and blessing till You come.

3. Child of our birth, child of our dying,
   fruit of the earth, breath of our sighing:
   we have grown weary, faith with excuses;
   fainting, we trust that You will come.

Words and Music:
Doug Constable
© 1975

12

SALTY LIGHT 4665

Words and Music: Doug Constable © 1996

Christ calls us salt, for we flavour the earth;
we savour with goodness, and season with worth.

Christ calls us light, for we shine through the world;
we brighten with goodness, illumine like gold.

Christ calls us blessed, for the cross we proclaim;
we witness love's goodness, and praise Jesus' name.

Christ, by your life, keep us salty and light,
forth-showing your goodness in all people's sight.

Father in heaven, let the good earth rejoice,
the whole world extol you, and thrive in your grace.

ART-SINGER
for Roderick Williams and Susie Allan

Led onto the stage by
an all-over smile that
declared his delight
that he had come to us,
that he would share
himself and would disclose
imagined tracks towards
far clearings, where tender
hearts meet freshly,
finding verdant understandings…

It turned out so.
Partnered by
a pianistic pastel-painter,
he brought us into spaces
where, each moment, we
might pitch emotions' camp
together. Too new for some,
too raw, he opened
sweeping love-lines and
vast griefs, while intimating
something pointed, awesome,
warm, completely safe…

not unlike
that carpenter one
synagogue-day, who
taught his friends and neighbours, family,
gracefully
to suck God's eggs…

His beauty undeniable,
his music was not wanted,
older favourites being preferred.

Still in the world,
his new songs heard,
he disempowers
our moral entropy,

while rising, resting
in praise.

19.8.15

13

Christ is the Lord of the smallest atom,
Christ is the Lord of outer space,
Christ is the Lord of the constellations,
Christ is the Lord of every place!
Of the furthest star, of the coffee bar,
of the length of the Berlin Wall,
of the village green, of the Asian scene,
Christ is the Lord of all!
Christ is the Lord of the human heartbeat,
Christ is the Lord of every breath,
Christ is the Lord of a man's existence,
Christ is the Lord of life and death.

Christ is the Lord of our thoughts and feelings,
Christ is the Lord of all we plan,
Christ is the Lord of a man's decision,
Christ is the Lord of total man!
In the local street where the people meet,
in the church, or the nearby hall,
in the factory, in the family,
Christ is the Lord of all!
Christ is the Lord of our love and courtship,
Christ is the Lord of man and wife,
Christ is the Lord of the things we care for,
Christ is the Lord of all our life.

Colossians 1.15-20
This is the first hymn lyric for which I composed music. Robin Morrell, whose curate I was, found these words written by a vicar from the other side of our city in a church newspaper, and, suggested the tune of the first line. Our congregation sang it with verve and gladness. There are obvious ways in which the text, written for the author's church youth club, is now dated, yet the hymn in itself still lives.

Kenneth Preston 1916-2012

Doug Constable
© 1968

MORRELL 10 8 10 8 5 8 5 5 10 8 10 8

♩. = 60

With a bounce

1. Christ is the Lord of the small-est a-tom, Christ is the Lord of out-er space, Christ is the Lord of the con-stel-la-tions, Christ is the Lord of ev'-ry place! Christ is the Lord of ev'-ry place!

2. Christ is the Lord of our thoughts and feel-ings, Christ is the Lord of all we plan, Christ is the Lord of a man's de-cis-ion, Christ is the Lord of to-tal man! Christ is the Lord of to-tal man!

Of the furth-est star, of the cof-fee bar, of the length of the
In the lo-cal street where the peo-ple meet, in the church or the
Ber-lin Wall, of the vil-lage green, of the
near-by hall, in the fac-tor-y, in the
As-ian scene, Christ is the Lord of all!
fam-i-ly,
Christ is the Lord of all.

Christ is the Lord of the hu-man heart-beat, Christ is the Lord of ev'-ry breath, Christ is the Lord of a man's ex-ist-ence, Christ is the Lord of life and death, Christ is the Lord of life and death!

Christ is the Lord of our love and court-ship, Christ is the Lord of man and wife, Christ is the Lord of the things we care for, Christ is the Lord of all our life, Christ is the Lord of all our life!

14

Doug Constable © 1997
GRACEGRAZING 87877
♩ = 76 Verses 1-2 UNISON

J.S.Bach 1685-1750
arranged by DC

1. Christ our shepherd, all souls calling, from the dead world to the live, each resisting lost sheep hauling, through their fears till grace revive.

2. Once life's way was all disputed, mined, and dumped on, closed to all. You went down, and hell uprooted, cleared our way for safe footfall.

HARMONY

3. Now the way through death lies open! Now abundant life is free! Now earth's commonwealth in hoping life's believers in your praise all cause to be.

4. Christ our shepherd, all souls' pastor, guard and guide at ev'ry turn: by your grace all fears we'll master, in your praise all joy we'll learn.

Christ our shepherd, all souls calling
from the dead world to the live,
each resisting lost sheep hauling
through their fears, till grace revive,
through their fears, till grace revive.

Once life's way was all disputed,
mined, and dumped on, closed to all.
You went down, and hell uprooted,
cleared our way for safe footfall,
cleared our way for safe footfall.

Now the way through death lies open!
Now abundant life is free!
Now earth's commonwealth-in-hoping
life's believers cause to be,
life's believers cause to be.

Christ our shepherd, all souls' pastor,
guard and guide at every turn:
by your grace all fears we'll master,
in your praise all joy we'll learn,
in your praise all joy we'll learn.

John 10.1-10; 1 Peter 2.19-25; Acts 2.42-47
Shortly before this text was written, Princess Diana publicly gave her backing to the campaign to ban landmines. The hymn's lyric is carried by Bach's much-loved melody. Underlining the obvious, the first two stanzas are deliberately set growlingly low in the voice, partly to express the predicament of we human 'sheep', and partly to highlight, in the following stanzas, the uplift imparted by Christ's resurrection.

15

Words (adapted from *Dies Sacerdotalis 1888*)
and Music: Doug Constable © 2007

♩ = 112 With a lilt

1. Come, Flaming Fire of Divine Love, burn up, come burn up my deadly wounds. Cleanse me, O cleanse me, that I may cleanse others. Enlighten me, enlighten me, that I may enlighten others. O
2. Come, Flaming Fire of Divine Love, burn up, come burn up our deadly wounds. Cleanse us, O cleanse us, that we may cleanse others. Enlighten us, enlighten us, that we may enlighten others. O

36

This prayer was set to be a congregational song, and to mark the ordinations
in Truro, of Rosalind Paul, and in Coventry, of John Horton.

16

Come, let me grow to know my Father's business!
See how I yearn to learn of heaven, and no less!
Share now my care, and dare to bear love's true cross!
    Bless God, who comes to save.

Come, let your child grow wild for peace and justice!
See how your youth learns truth that fruits in goodness!
Share in ripe age love's rage at sin's sick practice!
    Bless God, who dies to save.

Come, let your heart impart our Father's business;
See life's full worth, give birth to heaven's new witness;
Share every day love's way that comes to fullness;
    Bless God, who lives to save.

Words: Doug Constable © 2012
Music: CHRISTE SANCTORUM
from Paris Antiphoner 1681
Metre: 11 11 11 5

Luke 2.41-52 esp.v.49
This lyric responds to the story of the twelve-year old Jesus in the temple, in the midst of learned elders, both hearing them, and asking them questions.

An Easter Ditty: Changing The Agenda

This world's a sad and sorry sphere,
for hurt and hate breed freely here;
now raise a counter-intuitive cheer,
for Christ has grabbed the agenda ...

We Eves and Adams do our best,
though cuckoo-sin fouls up the nest;
but phoenix-love consumes the pest,
as Christ upends the agenda ...

Life's change-to-come is here today,
and longed-for peace is making its way,
new colours supplant decaying grey,
as Christ makes good the agenda ...

For Paschal Easter's a marriage-feast
where north and south weds west and east,
where old grow young, where last come first,
where love heals all. No labour's lost
where Christ is earth's befriender
and humpty-dumpty's mender,
embracing every gender,
where power is always tender ...

3.4.2021

17

ST.FINNIAN 11 10 10 10 12

Words and Music
Doug Constable
© 1995

♩ = 104

1. Come, make way for the music that sires the stars, make way for the silence that births the years, make way for the yearning that forms each name, make way for the heart-beat that calls us home, make way for the highest, the highest among us.

2. Come, make way for the neighbour who takes your hand, make way for the stranger who shares your land, make way for the cast-offs who carry our pain, make way for the helpless who suffer disdain, make way for the lowest, the lowest among us.

3. Come, make way for the leaven that raises bread, make way for the Spirit to rouse the dead, make way for the host who embraces the lost, make way for the last who will surely be first, make way for the fullness, the fullness among us.

4. Come, make way for our bodies with joy to bound, make way for our voices as thanks resound, make way for a ferment of passion and praise, make way for fomenting of love always, make way for the glory, the glory among us.

(Come, O come make way)

Come, make way for the music that sires the stars
    make way for the silence that births the years
    make way for the yearning that forms each name
    make way for the heartbeat that calls us home
    make way for the highest, the highest among us.

Come, make way for the neighbour who takes your hand
    make way for the stranger who shares your land
    make way for the cast-offs who carry our pain
    make way for the helpless who suffer disdain
    make way for the lowest, the lowest among us.

Come, make way for the leaven that raises bread
    make way for the Spirit to rouse the dead
    make way for the host who embraces the lost
    make way for the last who will surely be first
    make way for the fullness, the fullness among us.

Come, make way for our bodies with joy to bound
    make way for our voices as thanks resound
    make way for a ferment of passion and praise
    make way for fomenting of love always
    make way for the glory, the glory among us.

In autumn 1995 the Diocese of Winchester held a festival called *Make Way*, and I was invited to write a hymn for it. Only afterwards did I learn that Graham Kendrick had written a strong and joyful hymn with that name, and I realized that probably the festival was named after his song.

COMFORTER

Whose fanned wings blew the dust away,
whose song starts forth from where she soars before,
who spritely gashes the clouds with flame,
whose diving trail is light-fall in my eyes:

she brought me light in eyes
that never really looked on now
till now
when, windfall, she
within, without my window
winged her way,

and dropped the food of love you share with me.

          1976

18

"Companion me, and eat my bread",
the host to his disciples said;
"Commune with me, and drink my wine;
then you will share my life divine.

"Be one with me, feed on my flesh,
and drink my blood; I will refresh
to lasting life each faithful soul
who keeps my memory warm and whole.

"I am much more than humankind:
in drop and crumb you will me find.
Once I was bound to time and place;
my body now bears every face.

"And every day you take the strain
that wears you down, until again
you turn to me; then is my care
with bread and wine to greet you there."

Dear Jesus, when we come back home,
you meet us as a honeycomb
where every creature is restored
through fellowship with love's own Lord.

You are from heaven, God's living bread,
you show the truth, you raise the dead.
We, 'til you come, your death proclaim;
in Spirit one, we praise your Name.

Genesis 14.18-20; 1 Corinthians 11.23-26; John 6.52-58
A meditation on these three Scriptural texts, this hymn for the Feast of Corpus Christi (Thanksgiving for Holy Communion) is essentially a love-song in the medieval tradition of 'Jesu, thou joy of loving hearts … from the best bliss that earth imparts we turn unfilled to thee again… '
The music is named in gratitude for a friend whose living illuminated the' to-and-fro of love' in heaven and earth.

Words and Music
Doug Constable © 2002

VERNEY LM

♩ = 104 Gently, expressively, very smoothly

mp 1. Com - pan - ion me, and eat my bread, the host to his dis - ci - ples said. Com - mune with me, and drink my wine; you turn to me; then is my care
2. me, feed on my flesh, and drink my blood; I will re fresh to last - ing life each faith - ful soul comb, where ev' - ry creat - ure is re - stored
3. more than hu - man - kind: in drop and crumb you will me find. Once I was bound to time and place;
4. day you take the strain that wears you down, un - til a - gain
5. when we come back home, you meet us as a hon - ey -
6. heav'n God's liv - ing bread, you show the truth, you raise the dead. We, 'til you come, your death pro - claim;

then you will share my life di - vine, _____ then you will
who keeps my mem'-ry warm and whole, _____ who keeps my
my bod - y now bears ev' - ry face, _____ my bod - y

___ with bread and wine to greet you there, _____ with bread and
___ through fell - ow - ship with love's own Lord, _____ through fell - ow -
___ in Spir - it one, we praise your Name, _____ in Spir - it

share my life di - vine. _____
mem' - ry warm and whole. _____
now bears ev' - ry face. _____

wine to greet you there. _____
ship with love's own Lord. _____
one, we praise your Name. _____

last verse to

2. Be one with
3. I am much
4. And ev' - ry

5. Dear Jes - us,
6. You are from

COMMISSION
for Brian Foxon (1936-2013), on being licensed as a Reader

These words about the Word
becoming flesh within the world:
speak them in the voice that is your own.

These deeds enacting Love
becoming actual in our lives:
do them with the truth that's yours alone.

Speak what you know – no need to pretend;
let yourself go – Jesus taught us to bend;
do it just so – that yourself you expend,
and God will be glorified in you.

Take nothing on trust – you've a mind to find out;
there's nothing you must – choose where there's least doubt;
go heaven or bust – put all fear to the rout,
and God will be glorified in you.

This Bride of Christ the Groom
becoming flesh within her womb:
take her to the hearth that is your own.

These words about the Word
becoming you within the world:
read them with the love that's yours alone,

and to God full sown all glory be shown.

1985

19

Daw llafn o haul dy wanwyn di	*A blade of your spring sunlight*
i godi llen y llwydni,	*will come to lift the mildew curtain;*
drwy ddafn o wlith, drwy eirlys gwyn,	*through a drop of dew, through a snowdrop white,*
mae grym d'oleuni gloywi.	*the strength of light is shining.*
Briallu mwyn ar ffridd ar ffos,	*Dear primroses, in field and ditch*
a'r brigau brau'n blaguro;	*put forth frail buds on the summits;*
wynebwn lygad haul dy ras	*facing the sunshine-eye of your grace,*
i weld yn eglur eto.	*we see again, our vision restored.*

    Cytgan   Chorus

Dal ni yn llygad yr haul,	*Hold us still in the eye of the sun,*
yn gynnes yng ngwres dy ras;	*warm in the heat of your grace;*
dal ni yng ngolau dy gariad di.	*keep us in light of your love.*

Drwy gawod haul dy wanwyn di	*Through a sun-shower of your spring*
dy ynni ymbelydra;	*your energy irradiates;*
cofleidia ni yn nisglair des	*embrace us in warm brightness*
y gwres a'n hadnewydda.	*that renews us.*
Dysg ni i fyw yn llewyrch haul	*Teach us to live in the lustrous sun,*
yr un sy'n llonni'n llwybrau,	*the one who cheers our pathways,*
gan adlewyrchu'r cariad sy'n	*to reflect the love that*
rhoi'r gwanwyn yn ein gwenau.	*puts springtime in our smiles.*

    Cytgan   Chorus

Pan gryna seiliau sicrwydd byd,	*When truth's foundations are shaken,*
a phan ddaw'r gwyll i'n gwyro	*when gloom comes to derail us,*
gogwydda ni at lygad haul	*turn us back to the eye of the sun,*
i dyfu'n dalsyth eto.	*so we grow upward again.*
Pelydrau'th ras sy'n treiddio'n bod;	*Rays of your grace penetrate our being:*
amsugnwn nerth dy gariad,	*we breathe in your love's strength,*
estynnwn haul dy wanwyn di	*extend your springtime-sunlight*
a'i ledu hyd dy gread.	*and spread it throughout your creation.*

    Cytgan   Chorus

In 2012 these words, by Siân Rhiannon, were set for the class in the National Eisteddfod in which a new hymn was to be composed. In my translation, the lyric, a sunny affirmation of God's love continually poured forth through the grace of creation, is slightly paraphrased.

Siân Rhiannon © 2012 Doug Constable © 2013

LÔN Y LLAN

♩. = 56 Canu'n rythmig. Rhythmically

1. Daw llafn o haul dy wanwyn di i godi llen y llwydni, drwy ddafn o wlith drwy'r eirlys gwyn, mae grym d'oleuni'n gloywi. Bri-allu mwyn ar ffridd a ffos, a'r brigau brau'n blaguro; wynebwn lygad haul dy ras i weld yn eglur eto.

2. Drwy gawod haul dy wanwyn di dy ynni ymbelydra; cofleidia ni yn nisglair des y gwresa'n hadnewydda. Dysgni i fyw yn llewyrch haul yr un sy'n llonni'n llwybrau, ganadlewyrchu'r cariad syn rhoi'r gwanwyn yn ein gwenau.

3. Pan gryna seiliau sicrwydd byd, a phan ddaw'r gwyll i'n gwyro gogwyddan ni at lygad haul i dy fu'n dalsyth eto. Pe-lydrau'thras sy'n treiddio'n bod; amsugnwn nerth dy gariad, estynnwn haul dy wanwyn di a'i ledu hyd dy gread.

CYTGAN Refrain
Dal ni yn lly-gad yr haul, yn gyn-nes yng ngwres dy ras; dal
ten.
rall.
ni yngngo-lau dy ga - riad di.
2.Drwy di.
3.Pan_
1.2.
3.
CYSONDEB
Harmony
1.Daw llafn o haul
1.Daw___ llafn o haul dy wan - wyn di i
ga - wod haul dy wan - wyn di dy
gry - na sei - liau sic - rwydd byd, a
Daw___ llafn o haul
go- di llen y llwyd - ni, drwy ddafn o wlith, drwy'r eir - lys gwyn, mae
yn - ni ym - be - ly - dra; cof - leid - ia ni yn nis - glair des y
phan ddaw'r gwyll i'n gwyr - ro go - gwy - dda ni at ly - gad haul i

grym d'o-leu - ni'n gloy - wi. Bri - all - u mwyn ar ffridd a ffos, a'r
gwres a'n had - new - y - dda. Dysg ni i fyw yn lle - wyrch haul yr
dy - fu'n dal - syth e - to. Pel - yd - drau'thras sy'n treidd - io'n bod; am-

bri - gau brau'n bla - gur - o; wy - ne - bwn ly - gad haul dy ras i
un sy'n llon - ni'n llwy - brau, gan ad - le - wyrch - u ca - riad sy'n rhoi'r
sug - nwn nerth dy ga - riad, es - tyn - nwn haul dy wan - wyn di a'i

ten. *ten.* CYTGAN
weld yn eg - lur e - to.
gwan - wyn yn ein ge - nau. Dal ni yn
le - du hyd dy gre - ad.

ly - gad yr haul, yn gyn - nes yng gwres dy ras; dal ni yng ngo - lau dy

1.2. | 2.Drwy | 3.rall.
3.Pan
ga - - riad di. 2.Drwy di.
3.Pan

20

Dear God, I pray you, save
my soul from bitterness:
let me be tender-hearted, brave;
instead of cursing, bless.

The world has bile to spare,
and I have fed its store;
let me be merciful, and bear
some poor soul's burden raw.

When Jesus was reviled,
he yielded to your will,
he prayed as your beloved child
for those who wished him ill.

Let me, with all who rage
against contempt and shame,
help heal the world, write a new page
with love that knows no blame.

Words: Doug Constable © 2018
Music: SOUTHWELL
from Psalmes 1579 Damon
Metre: SM

Matthew 5.21-26, 43-45; Luke 23.33-34a
This hymn was prompted by words written to his nephew by James Baldwin:
Don't let it make you bitter. The world's bitter enough. We've got to be better than the world.

21

Dear Source of Joy, whence love is spawned
and journeys to its last shalom,
You see all life with good adorned,
You call all creatures to Your home.

Your template forms each human heart
to be the world where love may dwell,
where none is lost or kept apart;
where all are welcome, all goes well.

There neither ignorance nor pain
can find a fear on which to feed;
nor can dull prejudice sustain
the lies from which cold hate can breed.

Yet, with our mothers' milk, all learn
to see love's gift as threat-come-near;
from friends and strangers, both, we turn,
and fall away from faith to fear.

Christ Jesus, friend, exemplar, lord,
a mother taught You to forgive;
whom You called 'dog' won faith's reward:
Your heart enlarged, her child could live.

So, into love's exclusive space,
we pray You, welcome sinners, all,
hospitably; pleased to embrace
the last-come-first who hear your call.

Words: © Doug Constable 2000
Music: EISENACH or MELCOMBE
Metre: LM

Matthew 15.21-28
Entered into a competition for a new hymn 'about inclusion', this was written with help from friends who experienced exclusion in their daily lives.

CRUCIFIXION EVENING

In the end
the very smell of life,
of death,
is gone.
The wind has carried all the cinder-seeds away.
The stake your pain-hot body charred:
a shriveled stump,
a pimple on the earth.

Long and low and endless is the whining of the void.
The life you sang is jammed by no sound
pierced into my mind.
This crucifixion
dark and deep and timeless is.

They say that, from the wood,
a bud will thrust and burst to flower,
that streams will spring at dawn,
that once again your feet will print
the road beyond this end.

Maybe.

I know there was a day
when you were all the joy and pain
before my eyes …

my eyes that rose on cross-tipped hills.

1974

22
GREAT GARDINER 77 77

Words and Music
Doug Constable
© 2001

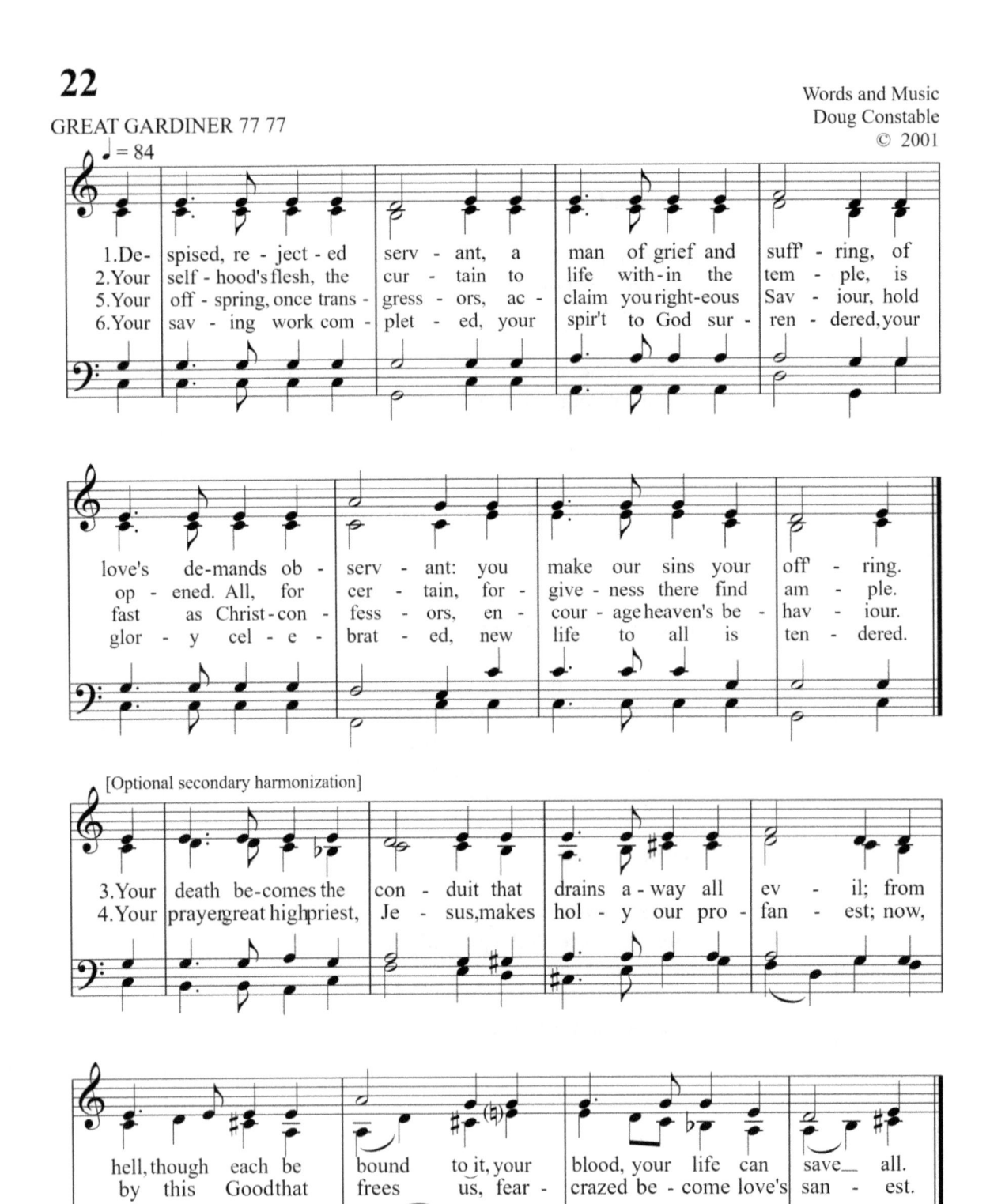

♩ = 84

1. Despised, rejected servant, a man of grief and suff'ring, of love's demands observant: you make our sins your off'ring.

2. Your selfhood's flesh, the curtain to life within the temple, is opened. All, for certain, forgiveness there find ample.

3. Your death becomes the conduit that drains away all evil; from hell, though each be bound to it, your blood, your life can save all.

4. Your prayer, great high priest, Jesus, makes holy our profanest; now, by this Good that frees us, fear-crazed become love's sanest.

5. Your offspring, once transgressors, acclaim you righteous Saviour, hold fast as Christ-confessors, encourage heaven's behaviour.

6. Your saving work completed, your spir't to God surrendered, your glory celebrated, new life to all is tendered.

[Optional secondary harmonization]

Despised, rejected servant,
a man of grief and suffering,
of love's demands observant:
you make our sins your offering.

Your selfhood's flesh, the curtain
to life within the temple,
is opened; all, for certain,
forgiveness there find ample.

Your death becomes the conduit
that drains away all evil;
from hell, though each be bound to-it,
your blood, your life, can save all.

Your prayer, great high priest, Jesus,
makes holy our profanest;
now, by this Good that frees us,
fear-crazed become love's sanest.

Your offspring, once transgressors,
acclaim you righteous Saviour,
hold fast as Christ-confessors,
encourage heaven's behaviour.

Your saving work completed,
your spirit to God surrendered,
your glory celebrated;
new life to all is tendered.

Isaiah 52.13-53.12; Hebrews 10.16-25; John 19.30-34.
An address, a prayer, to the crucified and glorified Christ. To the eyes of faith he is both the Suffering Servant and the Levitical High Priest who oversees the ceremonies of the Day of Atonement (see Leviticus 16). The music is intentionally dirge-like, echoing the 'Funeral March for a Hero' in Beethoven's Piano Sonata Opus 26. It is named for the Orthodox GREAT and Good Friday, and for Allen GARDINER (1794-1851), a missionary who died of starvation in Tierra del Fuego.

23

Doug Constable
© 1997

Trad. Welsh Lullaby
arr. DC

SUO GÂN 8787D

♩ = 80 Gently rocking

1. Do not let your hearts be troubled, neither let them be afraid,
though the fear of death surround you, though you be by loss dismayed.
You believe in God the Father, source of mercy and of grace:
now believe I go before you to prepare your heav'nly place.

2. Though I pass beyond all knowing, yet you know the way I go.
Though I leave all earthly being, I'll return, and bring you too.
I desire that you be with me, one within the Father's love.
You who see me, you've discerned the Father; you who ever, you've discerned the One above.

3. Do not let your hearts be troubled, let your spirits be restored.
Trust the way, the truth before you: life with God your sure reward.
Work today for deepest healing of the world's enduring woe;
I'll be with you in the Father; Love in all shall live and grow.

Do not let your hearts be troubled,
neither let them be afraid,
though the fear of death surround you,
though you be by loss dismayed.
You believe in God the Father,
lord of mercy and of grace:
now believe I go before you
to prepare your heavenly place.

Though I pass beyond all knowing,
yet you know the way I go.
Though I leave all earthly being,
I'll return, and bring you too.
I desire that you be with me,
one within the Father's love.
You who see me, you whoever,
you've discerned the One above.

Do not let your hearts be troubled,
let your spirits be restored.
Trust the way, the truth before you:
life with God your sure reward.
Work today for deepest healing
of the world's enduring woe;
I'll be with you in the Father;
Love in all shall live and grow.

John 14.1-14
These stanzas paraphrase part of Jesus' 'Farewell Discourse'. One day, when reading this Scripture, the first line sang itself in my mind to the first couplet of *Suo Gân,* so I wrote the rest of the text to fit that dear melody.

24

Robin Morrell (1929-2010)

Doug Constable
© 1969

STOCKHELSTON WOOD 88 87D CM D

♩ = 72 Mournfully

Down went Mary, down to the tomb, ver-y ear-ly, be-fore the day.
When she got there, where was the stone? Oh, the tears spring in-to her eyes!

1. She went sad-ly, nev-er glad-ly, to the gar-den all the way.
2. Weep-ing heart moans, ach-ing tired bones; now her last faint com-fort dies.

Quicker

John 20.11-18
Robin laid his words before me, with his sense that the chorus should evoke the Helston Floral dance. He also hoped our congregation would sing and dance the carol on Easter Morning. We didn't manage the dance, but the singing was appropriately joyful.

25

Words and Music
Doug Constable
© 1982

ALNMOUTH 10 10 10 10

♩= 148

1. From far away I hear you calling me: seeking to save, your voice is loud and clear. What shall I say? You know my frailty. "Fear not," you answer, "I your Lord am here."

2. Trembling I

From far away I hear you calling me:
seeking to save, your voice is loud and clear.
What shall I say? - you know my frailty.
"Fear not," you answer, "I your Lord am here."

Trembling, I yield my heart to your embrace,
not knowing whether I may live or die;
heaven in my arms, I dare to find your face:
in faith, I know you come from God on high.

Most royal Jesus, seated on your throne
beside me, searching all my life and love:
all that I am is yours to break and own;
unworthy servant, I your friend would prove.

And now you give what you command: my peace,
healing, and hope, my will to love new-charged.
Within my heart your Spirit works release:
my trust and strength is by your power enlarged.

Ascended Christ, be still my welcome guest;
though death removes you from our earthly sight,
my neighbour bears to me your presence blest;
we find each other in your heavenly light.

Salvation dawns within this house today!
See how your grace makes mercy in us all!
In truth your life directs us on our way
always to new horizons as you call.

Saviour, you came by water and by blood
to rule our lives that your dear love has won.
We praise you, crucified and risen Lord
in sovereign Godhead, Father, Spirit, Son.

Luke 19.1-10

This hymn was written with a forthcoming Derby Diocesan Mission in mind. It invokes a picture of Zacchaeus making Sacramental Confession to Jesus, who brings *salvation* to *this house today*. Words and music were written during a stay at the Friary in ALNMOUTH, Northumbria.

26

Liturgy of St James (Anonymous Greek)
trans. C.W.Humphreys (1840-1921)

Doug Constable
© 1976

ONUPWARDS 14 14 14 15

1. From glory to glory advancing, we praise Thee, O Lord. Thy Name, with the Father and Spirit be ever adored.

3. giving and glory and worship, and blessing and love, one heart and one song have the saints on earth and above.

V1 second time to CODA

2. From
4. Ever-

Mark 6.31-44

This setting was for a dramatic presentation at Lee Abbey about the Gospel of Mark. The feeding of five thousand men with five loaves and two fish is likened to fans of Cup Final underdogs finding their team three goals ahead with ten minutes to go

27

God's boundless Love, the universe enfolding,
upholding every creature great and small,
you bring earth joy, our wholesome future moulding,
and we adore you, Saviour, Friend of all.
We breathe heaven's air that daily swells with mercies,
we seethe in, feed on, your goodwill and care;
your body broken endless hope disburses,
and blood outpoured infuses faith to share.

O Tender Christ, pity our hard hearts hurting,
as we free others, let us be set free;
you bring earth joy, all debt-bound souls converting;
now we adore God's Saving Mystery.
The way before us opens into glory,
your light breaks forth and brightens every face;
you gather all into a new-world story,
and from the Cross you call to love's embrace.

Tune: DERRY AIR
Doug Constable © 2019

28

God, in-breathing Holy Scripture,
breathe your word into my soul,
penetrate my deepest darkness,
light my path, and make me whole.

God, forth-breathing Love's good purpose,
breathe your word through all the earth,
scour and cleanse the world's deep dungeons,
open doors, bring peace to birth.

God, Christ-breathing Word within us,
breathe the truth that makes us free,
rouse each soul to hope of glory,
raise our flesh to victory.

Words: Doug Constable © 2007
Music: GOTT WILL'S MACHEN
J.L.Steiner 1668-1761
Metre CM

2 Timothy 3.16-17
I wrote this to give wings to a sermon preached in St Teilo's Church Llandeilo Fawr on Bible Sunday (which is also Reformation Sunday in parts of the Protestant world).

29

Words and Music
Doug Constable
© 2018

MARTINSTAG 7777
♩. = 68

1. God, whose nature is to share, making mercy ev'rywhere: turn our hearts to common good, make us share our warmth, our food, make us share our warmth, our food.

2. Make us follow Martin's lead, heed, and answer others' need; moved, he halved his soldier's cloak: make us share our own good luck, make us share our own good luck.

3. Make us face our foes unarmed, strong with love, that none be harmed, and, like Martin, brave the sword, bearing Christ, the peace-full Word, bearing Christ the peace-full Word.

4. Faith from God makes goodness thrive, Hope in God keeps truth alive, Love for God defeats all fear, Grace of God brings heaven near, Grace of God brings heaven near.

God, whose nature is to share,
making mercy everywhere:
turn our hearts to common good,
make us share our warmth, our food.

Make us follow Martin's lead:
heed, and answer others' need;
moved, he halved his soldier's cloak:
make us share our own good luck.

Make us face our foes unarmed,
strong with love, that none be harmed,
and, like Martin, brave the sword,
bearing Christ, the peace-full Word.

Faith from God makes goodness thrive,
Hope in God keeps truth alive,
Love for God defeats all fear,
Grace of God brings heaven near.

"Gott, dessen Wesen es ist, zu teilen,
Überall Mitleid zu üben:
Wende unsere Herzen zum Whole Aller,
Mach, das wir teilen: unsere Wärme, unsere Speise.

Mach, dass wir Martins Vorbild folgen:
Das Bedürfnis der Anderen bemerken und es erfüllen;
In Barmherzigkeit teilte er seinen Soldaten mantel:
Mach, das wir unseren eigenen Wohlstand teilen.

Mach, dass wir unseren Gegnern ohne Waffen entgegentreten,
Stark in der Liebe, das Niemandem Schaden zu gefügtwerde,
Und, wie Martin, dem Schwert trotzen,
Christus tragend, das Friedenswort.

Glaube, von Gottgeschenkt, lässt die Güteaufblühen,
Hoffnung auf Gott hält die Wahrheit lebendig,
Liebeim Namen Gottes vertreibt alle Furcht.
Gottes Gnade bringt den Himmel nah herbei."

Übersetzt von Günter Schlechter

This was written as a contribution to a celebration of St Martin on 11th November 2018 ('Martinstag') in the Roman Catholic parish of St Ansgar in Rendsburg, Schleswig, Germany. Günter Schlechter, the Director of the Church Choir, requested the hymn for the choir to sing, and he provided the accompanying translation for the congregation.

30

Words and Music
Doug Constable
© 2001

MIZEKI 777 777 66
♩ = 104

1. God, you look within the heart, scorning all cosmetic art,
finding ev'ry hidden part: help us choose what is to be,
nor resist your grace, but see Christ in ev'ry life set free, and
lift our lives with praise, and lift our lives with praise.

2. God, you see not with our eyes, judge not like the blindly wise,
bring all truth to light's surprise: in your will we find our rest,
welcoming your grace expressed: Christ, of heaven and earth the zest, whom
all our lives upraise, whom all our lives upraise.

3. God, when you anoint your own, pouring oil on David's throne,
you empower for life full-blown: we would be the souls you choose,
graced for service, to infuse Christ as all the world's good news, whose
cross all duties pays, whose cross all duties pays.

God, you look within the heart,
scorning self-deceiving art,
finding every hidden part:
> help us choose what is to be,
> nor resist your grace, but see
> Christ-in-every-land-set-free,
> and lift our lives in praise.

God, you see not with our eyes,
judge not like the blindly-wise,
You make good what we despise:
> in your will we find our rest,
> thriving in your grace expressed:
> Christ, of earth and heaven, the best
> whom all our lives upraise.

God, when you anoint a soul,
grows that half-formed spirit whole,
humbly turns towards life's goal:
> we would be the souls you choose,
> graced for service, to infuse
> Christ as all the world's good news,
> whose cross all duties pays.

1 Samuel 16.1-13; John 9.39
This hymn elaborates the story of David being anointed to be king (he was Samuel's eighth choice for the job). It also highlights Jesus' words, 'For judgement I came into this world, that those who do not see may see, and that those who see may become blind.'
The music, which moves by step (and should therefore be easy to learn), was written on the annual day of commemorating Bernard MIZEKI, Apostle of the MaShona, and Martyr.

31

Words and Music
Doug Constable
© 1997

HAMYSBOB 888
♩ = 100

1. He comes, unknown, to be baptised, out of the crowd, unrecognised, offers his being, undisguised.
2. He comes prepared to be revealed, body and soul to God will yield, offers his will: his choice is sealed.
3. He comes empowered, anointed, named: this is the Son by God acclaimed; offers himself, his life inflamed.
4. He comes immersed in God's desire, brings to the world love's judging fire, summons to faith till life expire.
5. You come; and, Christ, we'll go with you in and through, off'ring our lives to life made new.
6. We come, baptised, to us, who died, and lives restored, giving God's all, to be adored.

He comes, unknown, to be baptised,
out of the crowd, unrecognised,
offers his being, undisguised.

He comes prepared to be revealed,
body and soul to God will yield,
offers his will: his choice is sealed.

He comes empowered, anointed, named:
this is the Son by God acclaimed;
offers himself, his life inflamed.

He comes immersed in God's desire,
brings to the world love's judging fire;
summons to faith till life expire.

You come; and, Christ, we'll go with you
into the waters, in, and through,
offering our lives to life made new.

We come, baptised, to serve one Lord:
Jesus, who died, and lives restored,
giving God's all, to be adored.

Isaiah 42.1-6 Matthew 3.13-17
Christians read these Scriptures as boldly outlining the nature and character of one who will come to be called 'Christ'. In the Church's imagination, it is as if data were needed to answer the question, "Who is this who is here being revealed to the world?"
This music was composed the day Hannah Mary had her hair Bobbed.

32

Words and Music:
Doug Constable © 1989

FIRTH PARK 98 98

♩ = 100

1. Here we stand, we Christian people, bearing the wounds of Christ our God,
armed with the strength of saints and angels, firm on the ground that Jesus trod.

2. He, in the power of love baptismal, thanks on his lips, his heart on fire,
hungry for life, for truth, for freedom, wasted the ies of dark despair.

3. He, in the grief of friends' betrayal, thorns in his flesh, his silence bore,
took to the cross, gave good for evil, plundered all hell, left Satan spare.

4. Whom he forgave, all Christ empowered, bearing the scars of his campaign,
see him endure love's war in heaven, Calvary waged till the end of time.

Here we stand, we Christian people, bearing the wounds of Christ our God,
armed with the strength of saints and angels,
firm on the ground which Jesus trod.

He, in the power of love baptismal, thanks on his lips, his heart on fire,
hungry for life, for truth in freedom, wasted the armies of dark despair.

He, in the grief of friends' betrayal, thorns in his flesh, his silence bore,
took to the cross, gave good for evil, plundered all hell, left Satan spare.

Whom he forgave, all, Christ-empowered, bearing the scars of his campaign,
see him endure love's war in heaven, Calvary waged till the end of time.

See him command Archangel Michael summon the hosts of mercy rare;
see the pretenders, howling vengeance, fall to the earth, their cause expire.

Therefore we hold, where people suffer, angel guard with healing care,
fiercely forgiving, foes embracing, fuelled, reinforced by heavenly power.

People of God, be sober, watchful, strong in the faith, though evils devour;
close with corruption in high places, own the victory of God's desire.

We stand forth, we Christian people, bearing the wounds of Christ our God,
armed with the strength of saints and angels,
firm on the ground which Jesus trod.

High in the heavens they lift the praise-song, deep out of earth God's glories soar,
infinite space resounds the chorus: Love carries all, and life is sure!

Revelation 12.7-12
This was written at FIRTH PARK in Sheffield to be offered as a processional hymn for the church of St Michael the Archangel in Southampton City Centre. Someone commented, after our first singing of this hymn, that it was "like an Anglo-Saxon war-chant"; the reference being, presumably, to the image in The Dream of the Rood (an Anglo-Saxon poem), of *mankind's Lord ... The young hero stripped himself - he, God Almighty - strong and stout-minded. He mounted high gallows, bold before many ...*

FRESH SPRINGS
for Adrian SLG

I love the way that, in Psalm Eighty-seven,
    the life-affirming climax comes at last
(just like the wine at Cana's wedding-feast):

with Zion imaged, dancers sing of heaven,
   'All my fresh springs in thee' (at that repast,
when all had drunk, You drew forth wine, the best).

Now, here at home in heaven's Temenos,
        enclosed within high walls of holy love,
borne up on waves of practised prayer and praise,

   with all your body's herstory, your cross
   of daily thanks, your family, you prove
   this day to be as every day, always

a new birth into all that spring shall give:

the joy of Christ in bringing all alive.

October 2017

33

I am among you as one in danger,
I am among you as one escaping,
I am among you as one in hiding:
I am among you, all is well.
    Jesus beside in faith's asylum,
    Jesus beside in hope's sure haven,
    Jesus beside in love's full welcome:
    Jesus beside us, all is well.

I am among you as one surviving,
I am among you as one returning,
I am among you as one with others:
I am among you, all is well.
    Christ beside is life reviving,
    Christ beside, our way discerning,
    Christ beside our sisters and brothers:
    Christ beside us, all is well.

I am among you as one beseeching,
I am among you as one upholding,
I am among you as one inspiring,
I am among you, all is well.
    God beside, the soul of mercy,
    God beside, our spirits raising,
    God beside, the hope of glory,
    God beside us, all is well.

Matthew 2.13-23 Hebrews 2.14-18 and 13.12-16
This hymn offers a voice to Christ as refugee and companion-saviour of asylum-seekers in every age. Prompted by the story of the Flight into Egypt, its heart derives from Isaiah 63.9: *It was no messenger or angel but his presence that saved them; in his love and in his pity he redeemed them; he lifted them up and carried them all the days of old.*
The form of the hymn is a dialogue between Christ and the soul, the first voice being I AM, the second acknowledging "Jesus, Christ, God beside…"

Words and Music
Doug Constable
© 1996

RAYMOND

UNISON ♩. = 48 Smoothly. Whole-line phrases.

1. I am a-mong you as one in dan-ger,
2. I am a-mong you as one sur-viv-ing,
3. I am a-mong you as one be-seech-ing,

I am a-mong you as one es-cap-ing,
I am a-mong you as one re-turn-ing,
I am a-mong you as one up-hold-ing,

I am a-mong you as one in hid-ing,
I am a-mong you as one with oth-ers,
I am a-mong you as one in-spir-ing,

HARMONY

I am a-mong you: all is well.

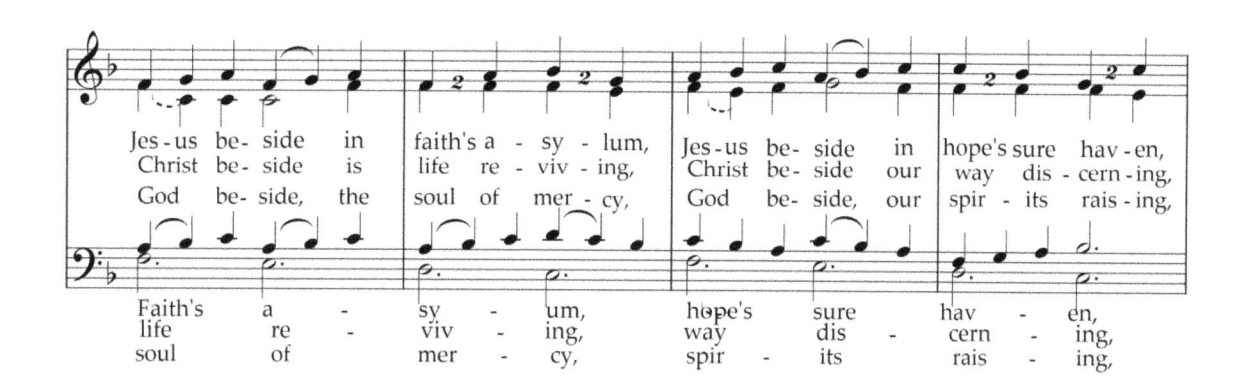

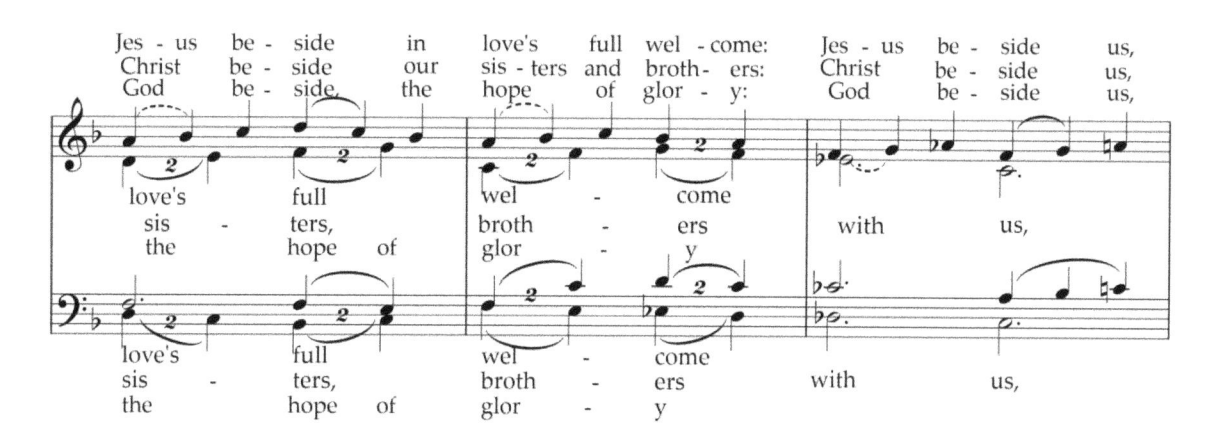

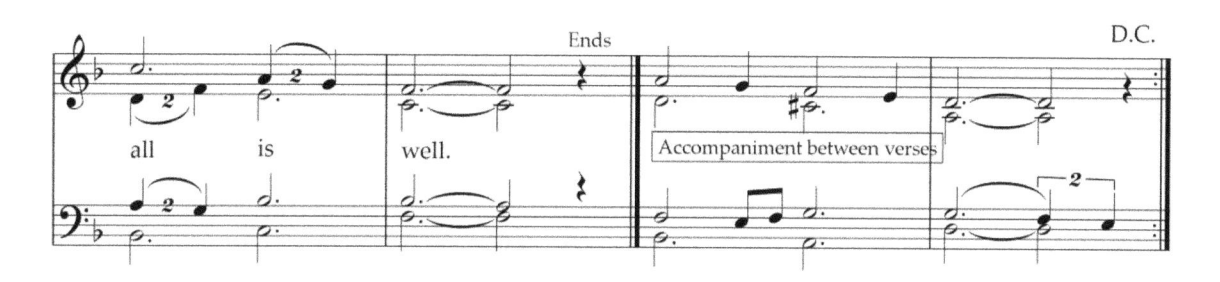

Jes-us be-side in faith's a-sy-lum, Jes-us be-side in hope's sure hav-en,
Christ be-side is life re-viv-ing, Christ be-side our way dis-cern-ing,
God be-side, the soul of mer-cy, God be-side, our spir-its rais-ing,

Faith's a-sy-lum, hope's sure hav-en,
life re-viv-ing, way dis-cern-ing,
soul of mer-cy, spir-its rais-ing,

Jes-us be-side in love's full wel-come: Jes-us be-side us,
Christ be-side our sis-ters and broth-ers: Christ be-side us,
God be-side, the hope of glor-y: God be-side us,

love's full wel-come
sis-ters, broth-ers with us,
the hope of glor-y

love's full wel-come
sis-ters, broth-ers with us,
the hope of glor-y

all is well.

Accompaniment between verses

D.C.

34

Words © 2003
and Music © 1973
Doug Constable

DWARNERJE 10 10 10 10 10 10
♩ = 108

1. 'I can-not look on Thee' to Love I said, 'al-though You gave my heart its eyes and head. I can-not think how I shall ans-wer Thee whom I of-fend, yet who gives grace to me.' But You lift up my heart, my fal-len year, and by Your Pre-sence emp-ty all my fears.

2. I have dis-dained the call on hu-mans laid, the call first heard by Is-ra-el a-fraid. They prayed You not to speak, lest they should die, while I de-ny Your right to rule this 'I'. In all You still ex-pose that awe-some dread, that none by sin, but each by Love be fed.

3. You wel-come means that all can live in peace, from en-vy, lust, in-dul-gence find re-lease. Your bless-ing heals, con-verts the dead-'ning heart, in-spires to hon-our all with court-eous art. You are our God, un-e-qualled sov-'reign Lord; by You all thrive; Your Name shall be a-dored.

4. Of this world's goods I have more than I need, for You sup-ply Christ's bread on which I feed. I wear with pride my free-dom from all shame, yet all is burned to ash in Christ's full flame. En-able me, with ev-'ry liv-ing soul, to rise with Christ, and see Your Love made whole.

The 1st, 3rd and 5th lines could be sung by different soloists. They could also be rendered in free time.

'I cannot look on Thee' to Love I said,
'although You gave my heart its eyes and head.
I cannot think how I shall answer Thee
whom I offend, yet who gives grace to me.'
But You lift up my heart, my fallen years,
and by Your Presence empty all my fears.

I have disdained the call on humans laid,
the call first heard by Israel afraid.
They prayed you not to speak, lest they should die,
while I deny Your right to rule this 'I'.
You still expose in all that awesome dread,
that none by sin, but each by Love be fed.

Your welcome means that all can live in peace,
from envy, lust, indulgence find release.
Your blessing heals, converts the deadening heart,
inspires to honour all with courteous art.
You are our God, unequalled sovereign Lord;
by You all thrive; Your Name shall be adored.

Of this world's goods I have more than I need;
for You supply Christ's bread on which I feed.
I wear with pride my freedom from all shame,
yet all is burned to ash in Christ's full flame.
Enable me, with every living soul,
to rise with Christ, and see Your Love made whole.

Exodus 20.1-4,7-9,12-20; Philippians 3.4b-14
'Love bade me welcome' wrote George Herbert (1593-1633), 'yet my soul drew back ...' Herbert was like the Israelites when God spoke to give them the Ten Commandments: they trembled and stood at a distance ... Verse three of this hymn shows that the Commandments are not (as is often supposed) a series of prohibitions, to stop people doing what they want, but were given for the right ordering of relations with God and our fellow creatures. The last verse echoes St Paul, who voluntarily suffered the loss of all things that (he might) know Christ and the power of his resurrection, and (might) share his sufferings.
The music was composed during a Lee Abbey Mission in Holy Epiphany Bournemouth, in the home of the parish priest and his wife, David and Jean WARNER.

35

Words and Music
Doug Constable
© 1975/2021

POLLOCK 11 10 11 10
♩ = 128 Smooth, flowing

1. Image and likeness of God is our union, born of Love's pleasure, achieved by Love's word; Godhead poured into our lives; flesh in our flesh, Love's dear blood for our body. Here is our love-life, and here is our Lord. Holy our maker, and holy our prize.

2. Moulded and fashioned for joy is our congress: peace from the passion of Christ on the tree, Spirit incarnate, whose work is our wholeness: Here is our love-life, and here is our Lord. Christ is our servant, and Christ sets us free.

3. Humbly we offer each other atonement, taught by the faithfully given, and broken, abandoned: Here is our love-life, and here is our Lord.

4. Image and likeness of God is our paradise, light of the new day breaks ever again! Building a temple of love through our body: end and beginning, all glory we claim!

Image and likeness of God is our union,
born of Love's pleasure, achieved by Love's word;
flesh in our flesh, Love's dear blood for our body:
Here is our love-life, and here is our Lord.

Moulded and fashioned for joy is our congress –
peace from the Godhead poured into our lives;
Spirit incarnate, whose work is our wholeness:
Holy our maker, and holy our prize.

Humbly we offer each other at-one-ment,
taught by the passion of Christ on the tree,
faithfully given and broken, abandoned:
Christ is our servant, and Christ sets us free.

Image and likeness of God is our paradise –
light of the new day breaks ever again!
Building a temple of love through our body:
end and beginning, all glory we claim!

Ephesians 5.25-33
Written for a colleague's wedding in 1975, this was originally sung by a choir of (mostly young) women; hence the otherwise unthinkably high G flat in the last line. A vocally more accessible version, with words altered for gender equality, can be found in *Reflecting Praise,* jointly published by © Stainer & Bell and Women in Theology in 1993. The words were further revised in 2021.

36

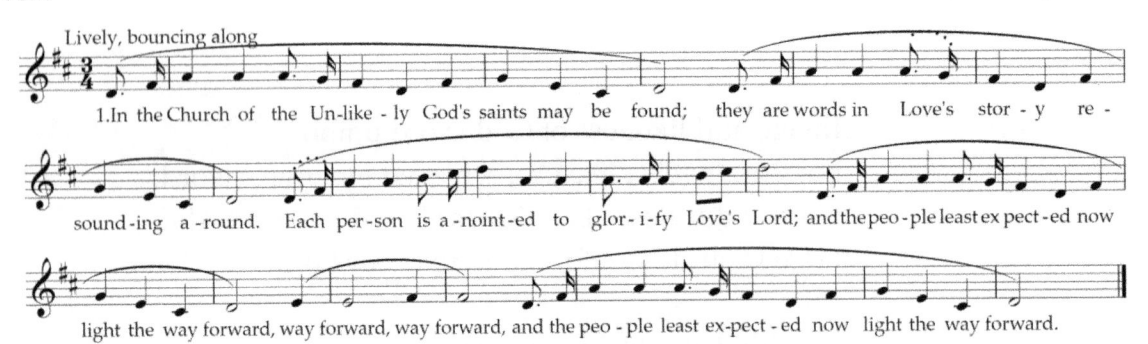

Words: Doug Constable
© 2001

Sans Day Carol
(19th century Cornish)

Lively, bouncing along

1. In the Church of the Unlikely God's saints may be found; they are words in Love's story resounding around. Each person is anointed to glorify Love's Lord; and the people least expected now light the way forward, way forward, way forward, and the people least expected now light the way forward.

In the Church of the Unlikely God's saints may be found;
they are words in Love's story resounding around.
Each person is anointed to glorify Love's Lord;
and the people least expected now light the way forward,
　　way forward, way forward,
and the people least expected now light the way forward.

In the Church of the Unlikely the last become first,
and the silenced find their voices, fear's bubble gets burst.
Each person is appointed to magnify Love's Lord;
and the people least respected are brightness outpoured,
　　outpoured, outpoured,
and the people least respected are brightness outpoured.

In the Church of the Unlikely live fools for Christ's sake;
they are noisy, they are nosey: fear's bondage they break.
Each person fitly-jointed to tumble for Love's Lord;
and the people least projected to heights are now soared,
　　now soared, now soared,
and the people least projected to heights are now soared.

In the Church of the Unlikely the Sp'rit is not quenched;
charismatic, and ecstatic, by Love folk get drenched.
Each person is acquainted with Jesus and Love's Lord;
and the people least accepted sit right at heav'n's board,
　　heav'n's board, heav'n's board,
and the people least accepted sit right at heav'n's board.

In the Church of the Unlikely the Trinity's all;
one for all, and all for each one, and upward the call.
Each person integrated, embodying Love's Lord:
Mother-Father, Son-and-Daughter, in Spirit's accord,
　　accord, accord,
Mother-Father, Son-and-Daughter, in Spirit's accord.

Matthew 11.25; 20.16; 23.12
Two Bible stories provide the background to this hymn: the choice of David (the eighth choice) to be king, in 1 Samuel 16.1-13, and, by spreading mud in his eyes, Jesus' giving sight to a man born blind, in John 9. The hymn is therefore a meditation on Jesus' saying *the first shall become last, and the last first*.
Worshipping congregations might think it appropriate to offer this hymn with as little dignity as possible!

37

In this dark world, unending Light
kindles a spark to brighten our night.
Hark to the Saviour, born in plain sight:
    Christ is made flesh among us.

Christ, we conceive you deep in our heart;
help us receive the life you impart;
may we perceive in you our new start,
    Word becoming flesh among us.

Christ, we embrace you all of our days;
ours be the face of your being always;
may we emblazon your name with praise,
    Truth becoming flesh among us.

Christ, we affirm you through all the world!
Peoples acclaim you, Hope unveiled!
Redeem us, one and all, Blest Child,
    Grace becoming flesh among us.

Born in each clime, the Word out of Heaven!
Born Light sublime, through whom Life is given!
Borne forth in time, Breath, Bread, love's leaven!
    God made flesh is now among us!

John 1.1-18
A hymn for the Christmas season, especially for the Feast of St John the Evangelist on 27th December.

Words and Music:
Doug Constable © 1998/2020

ST. VALERIE 99 97
♩. = 52 Flowing, smooth, whole-line phrases

1. In this dark world, unending Light
2. Christ, we conceive you deep in our heart
3. Christ, we embrace you all of our days;
4. Christ, we affirm you through all the world!
5. Born in each clime, the Word out of Heav'n!

[Bass]
1. In ... unending Light
2. Christ ... deep in our heart,
3. Christ ... all of our days;
4. Christ ... through all the world
5. Born ... Word out of Heav'n!

1. kindles a spark, to brighten our night.
2. help us receive the life you impart;
3. ours be your face of your being always;
4. May all acclaim you, Hope unveiled!
5. Born Light sublime, through whom Life is giv'n!

[Bass]
1. Christ ... brighten our night.
2. Christ, ... life you impart;
3. Christ ... joy always;
4. Christ ... Hope unveiled!
5. Through ... whom Life is giv'n!

[as T & B]
[alto]
1. Hark, hark, here in plain sight!
2. we see you our new start,
3. blaze your name with praise,
4. Redeem all, Blest Child,
5. Born Breath, Bread, love's leav'n!

[plus Tenor]
1. Hark to the Saviour, here in plain sight!
2. may we perceive in you our new start,
3. may we emblazon your Name with praise,
4. Redeem us, one and all, Blest Child,
5. Borne forth in time, Breath, Bread, love's leav'n!

1. Christ is made flesh among us.
2. Word becoming flesh among us.
3. Truth becoming flesh among us.
4. Grace becoming flesh among us.
5. God made flesh is now among us.

1. In this dark world, unending Light kindles a spark, to brighten our night. Hark to the Saviour, here in plain sight! Christ is made flesh among us.

2. Christ, we conceive you deep in our heart; help us receive the life you impart; may we perceive in you our new start, Word becoming flesh among us.

3. Christ, we embrace you all of our days; ours be your face of your being always; may we emblazon your Name with praise, Truth becoming flesh among us.

4. Christ, we affirm you through all the world! Peoples acclaim you, Hope unveiled! Redeem us, one and all, Blest Child, Word becoming flesh among us.

5. Born in each clime, the Word out of Heav'n! Born Light sublime, through whom Life is giv'n! Borne forth in time, Breath, Bread, love's leav'n! God made flesh is now among us.

[Last verse only *poco rit.*]
[Bottom F last verse only]

85

GOSPEL PROCESSION

The Gospel calls out from the heart of the altar,
telling of God sacrificed in a halter
of self-giving love, offered up as a lamb
for the life of the world. It's the kindling flame
of a brightening story that searches each heart;
it's the truth borne aloft; it proclaims a new start
for each adam-and-eve lifted out of their prison
to sing Hallelujah; for Christ is a-risen!

The Gospel goes forth to each home, hub, and highway,
it reaches for souls hid and lost in the by-way
of folly and pain, calling all to the feast
in the kingdom of heaven, for greatest and least.
The Gospel is love in its glory and grace
renewing old adam-and-eve face to face,
to praise the redeemer who fills up each prison
with loud Hallelujahs; for Christ is a-risen!

The Gospel is coming alive as a being
that's gloriously human, who's endlessly freeing
each creature in bonds, finding siblings to hand
in all peoples, and willing, with Jesus, to stand
at the cross-roads, disarming the devil with good,
all armoured with Spirit of God's own blood,
and praising the Lord out of death's long prison
with high Hallelujahs; for Christ is a-risen!

Holy Saturday 2019

38

Into a stream of passing days,
leaving a dream of live-long praise,
silently ebbs my soul away
into the drifting of my lost days.

Into the tide of passing years,
weaving a thread of grief-wrung tears,
silently seeps my blood away
into the draining of my lost years.

Into the deep springs love from high,
saving, befriending all who cry
(silently stirs my heart to pray):
into our longing comes God Most High.

Christ, could I reach you passing by!
Let me but touch your hem I cry!
Silently seek my soul today.
Christ, let me meet you, or else I die.

You will restore the flood-lost years,
you will dissolve all silting fears;
nothing shall more my faith dismay:
you are the shore to which life's boat steers.

Mark 5.25-34
This hymn has grown from a dance for a woman who had been haemorrhaging for twelve years.
The music is named after the woman who created the dance.

WALKER 88 88

Words and Music:
Doug Constable © 1974/2012

♩ = 88 Soft, tentative, gradually growing in confidence. The last verse fully confident.

SOLO or UNISON SOPRANOS

1. In - to a stream of pass - ing days,
2. In - to the tide of pass - ing years,
leav - ing a dream of live - long praise, sil - ent - ly ebbs my
weav - ing a thread of grief-wrung tears, sil - ent - ly seeps my
soul a - way in - to the drift - ing of my lost days.
blood a - way in - to the drain - ing of my lost years.

V3 STB hum. V4 STB Ah. V5 ALL: Words

3. Into the deep springs love from high,
saving, befriending all who cry
(silently stirs my heart to pray):
into our longing comes God Most High.

4. Christ, could I reach you passing by!
let me but touch your hem I cry.
Silently seek my soul today.
Christ, let me meet you, or else I die.

5. You will restore the flood-lost years;
you will dissolve my silting fears.
Nothing may more my faith dismay;
you are the shore to which life's boat steers.

39

RAMELTON 76 76 D

Words and Music:
Doug Constable
© 1996

1. I took the work you offered, all day the job you set; I thought you'd pay me something, I never dreamed I'd get the highest love that's given, a full and rich reward, a taste today of heaven, the saving power of God.

2. But then I felt offended and hurt, misunderstood: you latecomers as my equals? You'll pay them just as good your friend disagree, and tell me you'll always pay your friend

3. Though shame would overwhelm me for thinking to condemn, you all my fellow workers I'll share what grace supplies:

4. No less now will I offer, no more will I despise: with

I took the work you offered,
all day the job you set;
I thought you'd pay me something,
I never dreamed I'd get
> *the highest love that's given,*
> *a full and rich reward*
> *a taste today of heaven,*
> *the saving power of God.*

But then I felt offended
and hurt, misunderstood:
late-comers as my equals?
You paid them just as good
> *the highest love that's given &c*

Though shame would overwhelm me
for thinking to condemn,
you disagree, and tell me
you'll always pay your friend
> *the highest love that's given &c*

No less now will I offer,
no more will I despise:
with all my fellow workers
I'll share what grace supplies:
> *the highest love that's given &c*

Matthew 20.1-16
This hymn re-tells the parable of the Labourers in the Vineyard. Someone who had worked all day is at first annoyed with the employer, but is then moved to gratitude by the employer's generous spirit.
The music, conceived in the style of an Irish jig, was written shortly after visiting friends in RAMELTON, County Donegal.
Is this song really a hymn? If Sydney Carter's 'Lord of the Dance' is, then I think we can say this is too.

40

Words and Music 2006 & 2010
© Doug Constable

♩ = 96

1. It's time once more to turn to the door that leads with-in to a place where-in I am host and guest (like a bird in its nest), and all my care is to en-ter prayer.

2. Ap-proach-ing now, I breathe: see how! O Breath di-vine, in-breathing mine: pour me life's *chi*, pure en-er-gy, drench me in love flow-ing from a-bove.

3. My joys, de-lights, my days and nights, each grief, each groan to You is known. Let me not hide, but op-en wide to Your em-brace, O Heav'n-ly Grace.

4. Write on my heart with ten-der art Your will for me, my way to be. In-clude, en-fold each soul I hold most close, most dear; let none have fear.

5. En-large my heart to be more part of this Your world, that teems un-furled; if I hold back, make up my lack with kind-ly zeal; make love more real.

6. My words dry up; still fill my cup with Your own speech, to help me each day from this place, this bound-less space, turn forth with cheer, and find You near, share in love's prayer, here and ev'-ry-where.

It's time once more to turn to the door
that leads within to a place wherein
I am host and guest (like a bird in its nest);
and all my care is to enter prayer.

Approaching now, I breathe – see how!
O breath divine, in-breathing mine:
pour me life's *chi*, pure energy;
drench me in love flowing from Above.

My joys, delights, my days and nights,
each grief, each groan to You is known.
Let me not hide, but open wide
to Your embrace, O Heavenly Grace.

Write on my heart with tender art
Your will for me, my way to be.
Include, enfold each soul I hold
most close, most dear; let none have fear.

Enlarge my heart to be more part
of this Your world, that teems unfurled.
If I hold back, make up my lack
with kindly zeal; make love more real.

My words dry up; still fill my cup
with Your own speech, to help me each
day from this place, this boundless space,
turn forth with cheer, still find you near,
share in Love's prayer, here, everywhere.

This is a re-write of the poem written for Tabitha's ninth birthday, set to music four years later.
Chi is life-force, energy – Creator-Spirit

41

Words and Music:
Doug Constable
© 1996

CORRIS UCHAF 87 87
♩ = 84

1. Jesus Christ was handed over, judge of all, to be condemned;
   held his peace, spoke truth to power;
   victor, proved the victim's friend.

2. For his sake, still, thousands suffer, witness to their heav'nly Lord;
   speaking truth, with peace on offer,
   hold their confidence in God.

3. By your passion, Lord, you gather all the world in life's embrace,
   held in heaven by God our Father,
   stilled, transfigured, by love's peace.

4. Here we pray for all destroyers, victims all, and full of fear:
   free them to be life-defenders;
   let them hold your love most dear.

5. Spirit, send us forth rejoicing, doves for peace, and worldly-wise,
   all your saving will embracing,
   Christ's own life before our eyes.

Jesus Christ was handed over,
judge of all, to be condemned;
held his peace, spoke truth to power;
victor, proved the victim's friend.

For his sake, still, thousands suffer,
witness to their heavenly Lord;
speaking truth, with peace on offer,
hold their confidence in God.

By your passion, Lord, you gather
all the world in life's embrace,
held in heaven by God our Father,
stilled, transfigured, by love's peace.

Here we pray for all destroyers,
victims all, and full of fear:
free them to be life-defenders;
let them hold your love most dear.

Spirit, send us forth rejoicing,
doves for peace, and worldly-wise,
all your saving will embracing,
Christ's own life before our eyes.

John 18.19-23, 19.10-11 Acts 4. 8-12
This hymn, composed in CORRIS UCHAF, Powys, explores the paradox that in Jesus' arrest and trial
it is the prisoner who is judge, the victim who represents supreme authority. And Christ's passion is
universalised, so that innocent victims find grace to overcome their tormentors.

42

Jesus, light of heaven,
born a child on earth:
brighten all our darkness,
give the world new birth.

Not just nearby shepherds,
nor a chosen few,
but earth's farthest peoples
find their joy in you.

Not the star-struck only
not just rich, or wise,
but earth's poor and wretched
find in you life's prize.

Not just in a cradle,
nor in mother's gaze,
but in shame and dying
you receive our praise.

One with all earth's peoples,
past, and yet to be,
here I come to worship
Christ, who comes to me.

By your love's compassion,
through your faithful word,
evermore indwell us,
radiant Spirit-Lord.

Words: Doug Constable © 1996
Music: NORTH COATES
T.R.Matthews (1826-1910)
Metre: 65 65

Isaiah 60.1-6; Matthew 2.1-12
This simple prayer offers a voice to individual worshippers who may feel drowned out by the chorus of 'shepherds' and all others who seem to commandeer the ways we are supposed to 'do' Christmas.

Holy Week 1995

[1] In the beginning isness anded.
   Isness ands now.
   and shall be for ever glorying.

    And? Is
    that it? And? What's
    next? There must be more to life than and.

Isness saw and.
It was very good.
And isness rested.

Keep this day holy.

    [2] When Jesus saw the opposition he wept.
     "This was your day,
      and your knowing is still-born."
    And, king of penitents, he
    hired a donkey to the citadel, to
    drive out chrome and petrol dealers.

        "When you bray
         say: Our
         Father's in heaven,
        and
        we are to holify this day."

    Children and verily stones
    hosannaed; and lord macadam
    over-rolled the donkey down and in.
        Accomplished
        the glorious work.

            [3] In our and is our new beginning.

            And very early
            before the break of day
            isness rolled security away:
            "Not here, not there, not then, just
              Now
              the crucified."

        And I thought he was a street-cleaner. And
            then I heard my name
              garlanded with palms.

                Lazarus Saturday 1995

43

Words and Music:
Doug Constable
© 1994

CARRETTO 6554 5554

♩ = 84

1. Jesus, our sacrifice, heav'nly and human,
   here, though departed, silently we adore you.
   Brother, defender, teacher, and healer,
   friend of each creature: we adore you.

2. In simple melody, in deep'ning harmony,
   by word, and silently we adore you.
   In all our mem'ory, sharing, and testim'ny,
   in heart and tongue set free: we adore you.

3. Through all the universe, at hearth and cairn, the church
   raises the song of earth:
   Blessed Christ Jesus, by this, Your blood and cross
   wholly You've saved us.

Jesus, our sacrifice, heavenly and human,
here, though departed, we adore you.
Brother, defender, teacher, and healer,
friend of each creature: we adore you.

In simple melody, in deepening harmony,
by word, and silently, we adore you.
In all our memory, sharing, and testimony,
in heart and tongue set free: we adore you.

Through all the universe, at hearth and cairn, the church
raises the song of earth: we adore you.
Blessed Christ Jesus, by this, your blood and cross,
wholly you've saved us. We adore you.

This hymn was written to conclude a setting of the Stations of the Cross composed for the Anglican Parish of Southampton City Centre Parish in Holy Week 1994. The tune is named for Carlo CARRETTO, from whose popular biography 'I, Francis' we learn that St Francis of Assisi taught his friars, when entering a church, to say *We adore you, most holy Jesus Christ, here and in all your churches throughout the world.; and we bless you, because by your holy cross you have redeemed the world.*

**In memoriam Alan Kurdi (3)
found washed up on a beach in Turkey
and Galip (5), and Rehana, their mother.**

Breath, from whom all being breathes,
Love, in whom compassion seethes,
Friend, who rescues from despair:
God of mercy, hear our prayer.

Yesterday I lived at ease,
caring but myself to please;
now, see here a wasted child:
Lord, my heart grieves madly, wild!

He but one of thousands more
forced to flee the hand of war;
each a homeless refugee,
all in need of sanctuary.

Let us help them, one by one;
let them each be saved, bar none;
give us passion, give us power,
let us be a refuge-tower.

Christ in joy, and Christ in pain,
bearing every soul's worst strain,
lay your hands on all who fear,
may they know you're with them here.

Breath of new life from the old,
Love inspiring actions bold,
Friend at hand when sinners fall:
God, make mercy in us all.

6-10 September 2015

44

Jesus says: Here am I way up high –
What shall I do for a body?

We will be your body, Jesus,
we will carry you around,
we will be your workers, Jesus,
everywhere the need is found.

We will use our heads for Jesus,
we will think about his word,
we will speak the truth for Jesus,
everything we ever heard.

We will use our eyes for Jesus,
we will try not to be blind,
we will see the love of Jesus
everywhere we look and find.

We will use our hands for Jesus,
finding lots of things to do;
we will feel the power of Jesus:
everything that's old is new!

We will use our feet for Jesus,
trav'lling where he wants to go;
we will bring the news of Jesus
everywhere both high and low.

Jesus says: One more thing: will you sing
praises as one single body?

We will sing your praises, Jesus,
we will show you that we care;
we will stay united, Jesus,
here and now and everywhere.

I Corinthians 12.27-30
This was written for a joint Baptist and Anglican Young People's Holiday Club at Stockwood, Bristol, and sung there merrily every day for a week.

Words and Music
Doug Constable
© 1969
LADMAN 98 CM
♩= 108
Jes- us__ says, "Here am I__ way up__ high: whatshall I do for a____ bod -
y? two! three! four! five! six! seven! 1.We will beyour bod - y, Jes- us!
[SHOUT]
Jes - us!
We will car-ry you a- round,
We will thinka bout his word,
We will be your workers, Jes us!
We will speakthe truth for Jes us!
ev' - ry-wheretheneed is found.
ev' - ry-thing we ev - er
1.
2.Wewilluseourheads for

found.

3. We will use our eyes for Jes-us, we will try not to be blind; We will see the love of Jes-us, ev'-ry-where we look and find.

4. We will use our hands for Jes-us, find-ing lots of things to do; we will feel the power of Jes-us! ev'-ry-thing be-comes as new!

5. We will use our feet for Jesus, trav'-ling where he wants to go; we will bring the news of Jesus ev'-rywhere both high and low.

6. Jesus says, "One more thing: will you sing praises as one singing le-bod-y? TWO! THREE! FOUR!

FIVE! SIX! SEVEN! We will sing your prais-es, Jes - us! We will show you that we

2nd time: a semitone higher (B major)

care! We will stay u-nit - ed, Jes - us, here and now and ev'ry

where. We will sing your prais - es,

here and now and ev' - ry - where!

45

Doug Constable © 1997

BUNESSAN trad. Irish Gaelic
arr. DC

MORNING AMENDED 10 9 10 9

♩ = 76

1. 'Jesus' they named you, 'Master' they called you, and they defamed you: "Friend of the poor! Then they acclaimed you 'Son of the Highest'. Death has not tamed you, Lord evermore.

2. Once merely local, man of the moment, rode on a donkey, hung on a tree, now multifocal in ev'ry culture of your life's off'ring; you're universal; life is set free.

3. Sov'reign Compassion poured from the heavens, neighbours and nations seek for your path. Grant us expression of peace between peoples; love's good confession rises from earth.

4. Christ, we salute you, first among equals, and we entreat you: make us anew. May we build fruitful peace between peoples; let ev'ry creature flourish with you.

106

'Jesus' they named you, 'Master' they called you,
and they defamed you: 'Friend of the poor!'
Then they acclaimed you 'Son of the Highest';
death has not tamed you, Lord evermore.

Once merely local, man of the moment,
rode on a donkey, hung on a tree,
now multi-focal in every culture:
you're universal; life is set free.

Sovereign Compassion poured from the heavens,
neighbours and nations seek for your path.
Grant us expression of your life's offering;
love's good confession rises from earth.

Christ, we salute you, first among equals,
and we entreat you: make us anew.
May we build fruitful peace between peoples;
let every creature flourish with you.

Ephesians 1.21
This hymn celebrates the feast of the Ascension of Christ, *far above all rule and authority and power and dominion, and above every name that is named, not only in this age but in the age to come.*
When I had completed the lyric, it sang itself to BUNESSAN (best known to 'Morning has broken'), but that didn't quite work, because that tune asks for words of lighter texture than those I had chosen.
So I slowed the music down, to give more space for thoughtful singing.

46

Words and Music
Doug Constable
© 1980

PEARTREE 11 11 11 12

1. Judge of all peoples, each nation, party, creed,
   Eternal Witness of ev'ry thought and deed:
   see, here are hearts filled with thanks, and grief, and shame
   for good and ill we've done, from love, in anger's flame.

2. Brother of each boy and girl, each woman, man,
   Christ Jesus, sharing in ev'ry life's full span:
   see, here are heads filled with pride, with tears, with pain
   from heat of conflict, cross, and warfare's scarring stain.

3. Spirit of mercy, of hope, of healing power,
   whose grace blooms softly, soft like the poppy's flower:
   see, here are souls needing strength of love applied
   to daily tasks of forging wholesome peace worldwide.

4. Warm God of seasons, of sun and wind and rain,
   in whom we flourish, and die, and rise again:
   bless us in sorrow, as here we start anew
   and pray 'Your Kingdom come on earth' like morning dew.

Judge of all peoples, each nation, party, creed,
Eternal Witness of every thought and deed:
see, here are hearts filled with thanks, and grief, and shame
for good and ill we've done, from love, in anger's flame.

Brother of each boy, and girl, each woman, man,
Christ Jesus sharing in every life's full span:
see here are heads filled with pride, with tears, with pain,
from heat of conflict, cross, and warfare's scarring stain.

Spirit of mercy, of hope, of healing power,
whose grace blooms softly, soft like the poppy flower:
see, here are souls needing strength of love applied
to daily tasks of forging wholesome peace worldwide.

Warm God of seasons, of sun and wind and rain,
in whom we flourish, and die, and rise again:
bless us in sorrow, as here we start anew
and pray 'Your kingdom come on earth' like morning dew.

Suitable for any time of year, this was written with Remembrance-tide especially in mind.

47

OCTAGONAL

Words amd Music
Doug Constable
© 1972

Let there be peace on the earth, and let it be-gin with me; for peace is born on the earth, now let it be seen in me.

1. I bring you peace who are far from God, I bring you peace who are near. So join your lives in the peace of God: give peace to ev'ry-one here.

2. I bring you peace to build love from hate, I bring you peace from your fear. So join your hands for it's get-ting late: make peace to ev'ry one here.

3. I bring you peace through my flesh and blood, I bring you peace that is dear. So join with me in the peace of God: share me with ev'ry-one here.

REFRAIN D.C.

Let there be peace on the earth
and let it begin with me
for peace is born on the earth
now let it be seen in me.

I bring you peace who are far from God
I bring you peace who are near
so join your lives in the peace of God
give peace to everyone here.
    Let there be peace &c

I bring you peace to build love from hate
I bring you peace from your fear
so join your hands, for it's getting late
make peace with everyone here.
    Let there be peace &c

I bring you peace with my flesh and blood
I bring you peace that is dear
so join with me in the peace of God
share me with everyone here.
    Let there be peace &c

Ephesians 2.13-19
I had received a card inscribed "Let there be peace on earth and let it begin with me." At the time I was composing a musical Nativity tableau for members of the Lee Abbey Community in Devon, and I set these words to be the first words of the new-born Christ. Some years later I learned that they came originally from a song by Sy Miller and Jill Jackson.

48

KENOTIC 12 10 15 20

Words and Music
Doug Constable
© 2001

Let this mind be in me that was in Christ Jesus: humbled, obedient to death on a cross. (acc.) [last time] death on a cross.

1. Formed of the being of God, and embodying the nature divine, in the world born to serve, love untold came to save, put his body and blood on the line. Let this
2. Named and exalted by God, as the highest in heaven and earth, he gave all without loss, and enduring the cross, he leads sinners through death to new birth. Let this
3. Tombed by the lowest by God, with old Adam and Eve, one and all, he will lead us on high, till as Lord by and by, ev'ry creature bows down at his stall.

Let this mind be in me that was in Christ Jesus:
humbled, obedient to death on a cross.

Formed of the being of God, and embodying the nature divine,
in the world born to serve, Love untold came to save,
put his body and blood on the line.

Let this mind be in me that was in Christ Jesus:
humbled, obedient to death on a cross.

Named and exalted by God as the highest in heaven and earth,
he gave all without loss and, enduring the cross,
he leads sinners through death to new birth.

Let this mind be in me that was in Christ Jesus:
humbled, obedient to death on a cross.

Tombed with the lowest by God, with old Adam and Eve, one and all,
he will lead us on high, till as Lord by and by,
every creature bows down at his stall.

Let this mind be in me that was in Christ Jesus:
humbled, obedient to death on a cross.

Isaiah 49.1-4; Philippians 2.5-11
The Second Servant Song and the Hymn to the Kenotic Christ give the background to this hymn for Palm Sunday.

Lord, with each breath I take
you enter in my soul;
in breathing out, you make
me see the world made whole.

I see the world made whole
by breathing in your love;
you press upon my soul,
your love for all to prove.

To prove your love for all
with every passing breath,
I answer your clear call
to will my ego-death.

O let my ego live
and bond with your dear poor;
together we will thrive
and knock on heaven's door.

At heaven's door we'll breathe
the air of holy love
and serve each other, seethe
in healing from above.

The healing sun and rain
fall on earth's cross of fear;
Christ, breathe away our pain
with resurrection cheer.

Your rising breath brings cheer
to help the world grow whole;
thank you, love-ever-near
inbreathing each poor soul.

11.8.2019

49

Life, life, eternal life!
I'm looking for the life of the world to come.
I stopped going my way,
don't bother with the byway;
I'm moving, oh I'm moving,
yes I'm moving up the highway to kingdom come.

Christian cried with a voice of fear,
"How shall I escape when the judgement is near?
It's getting very late, and I mustn't wait; I'll go
straight on the way to the narrow gate, singing,
Glory to God in the highest! x2   *Life, life &c*

Christian carried a burden cruel:
weighed him down to the depths of his soul.
He ran to a place where there stood a cross
where he found him rest, and his load he lost by the
death of the Lord in the highest. x2   *Life, life &c*

Christian climbed up a difficult hill,
met new friends who re-armed his will.
He came to the vale where a monster dwelt;
he assailed the fiend, and defended himself, singing,
Holy is God in the highest! x2   *Life, life &c*

Christian passed through the Valley of Death,
he praised the Saviour with all of his breath,
then he took a short cut, but his way was out:
he got caught by despair in the Castle of Doubt, singing,
Help me, O God in the highest! x2   *Life, life &c*

Christian carried the Promise of Life,
and hastened forth from the prison of strife.
Now he beheld the City of Gold;
and the bells sang aloud for the pilgrim bold, ringing,
Heaven with God in the highest! x2   *Life, life &c*

This was written to be the theme-song for a Children's Holiday Club at St Thomas' Derby. It is a simple summary of Bunyan's *Pilgrim's Progress*. Though plainly a song, the piece is suitable as a hymn for all-age worship.

Words and Music
Doug Constable © 1981

BUNGRIM

Life, life, eternal life! I'm looking for the life of the world to come. I stopped going my way, don't bother with the by-ways: I'm moving, oh, I'm moving, yes, I'm moving up the highway to kingdom come!

1. Christian cried with a voice of fear, "How shall I escape when the judgement is near? It's getting ver-y late, and I mustn't wait, I'll go straight on the way to the nar-row gate, sing-ing, GLOR-Y TO GOD IN THE HIGH - EST! GLOR-Y TO GOD IN THE HIGH - EST! mov-ing up the high - way, I'm mov-ing up the high - way, I'm mov-ing up the high - way to king - - dom come!

Hebrews 13.12-15

50

Words and Music
Doug Constable © 1974

♩ = 100 Whole-line phrases

1. Looking at you, longing to give you all that I am, longing to lay my life in your hands, I see you looking at me.
2. Looking at you, feeling your eyes search all that I am, feeling you find the shame in my hands, I see you looking at me.
3. Looking at you, knowing you know the past that I am, knowing the future's out of my hands,
4. Looking at you, giving yourself to me as I am, giving your life to hold in my hands, I see you welcoming me. ends
5. Christ, at your birth, loving, renewing me as I am, loving, and forming love in my hands, I see you welcoming me.

Looking at you,
longing to give you all that I am,
longing to lay my life in your hands,
I see you looking at me.

Looking at you,
feeling your eyes search all that I am,
feeling you find the shame in my hands,
I see you looking at me.

Looking at you,
knowing you know the past that I am,
knowing the future's out of my hands,
I see you looking at me.

Looking at you,
giving yourself to me as I am,
giving your life to hold in my hands,
I see you looking at me.

Christ, at your birth,
loving, renewing me as I am,
loving, and forming love in my hands,
I see you welcoming me.

This was written to conclude a musical Nativity tableau at Lee Abbey, based on Luigi Santucci's imaginative biography *Wrestling with Christ* (1969 trans.1974). The scene is as in many a Christmas card: animals, shepherds and Magi – all creation indeed - worshipping in the stable; but with this difference, that the worshipper finds the Adored immediately and deeply already committed to them personally.

51

Words and Music
Doug Constable
© 1980

1. Looking for you, always, everywhere, longing for you, all my hoping to share, seeking each part for to heal and to bless, in ev'ry heart
2. Finding you here, all around, ev'rywhere, feeling the fear as I offer my care, touching your hand for to hold and caress (our worlds are spanned), I AM the endless
3. Ready to go with you all of the way, daring to grow closer every day: what we have done to the world we'll confess — that life is one.

pressure of love, endless pressure of love: all my pleasure is to treasure you in measureless love; and I'll die to awaken you to heaven, my love.

heaven, my love. heaven, my love.

120

Looking for you, always, everywhere,
longing for you, all my hoping to share,
seeking each part for to heal and to bless,
in every heart I AM the endless
> *pressure of love,*
> *endless pressure of love:*
> *all my pleasure is to treasure you*
> *in measureless love;*
> *and I'll die to awaken you for heaven, my love.*

Finding you here, all around, everywhere,
feeling the fear as I offer my care,
touching your hand for to hold and caress
(our worlds are spanned), I AM the endless
> *pressure of love &c*

Ready to go with you all of the way,
daring to grow closer every day:
what we have done to the world we'll confess –
that life is one. I AM the endless
> *pressure of love &c*

Song of Solomon 8.6 John 15.12-13
Juli Wills, Diocesan Youth Officer, requested a song for an All-Night Youth Vigil in Birmingham Anglican Cathedral. The theme 'Endless Pressure' was set by the young people.

52

Lord of all hopefulness, Lord of all joy,
whose trust, ever-childlike, no cares could destroy:
be there at our waking, and give us, we pray,
your love in our hearts, at the break of the day.

Lord of all eagerness, Lord of all faith,
whose strong hands were skilled at the plane and the lathe:
be there at our labours, and give us, we pray,
your strength in our hearts, Lord, at the noon of the day.

Lord of all kindliness, Lord of all grace,
your hands swift to welcome, your arms to embrace,
be there at our homing, and give us, we pray,
your love in our hearts, Lord, at the eve of the day.

Lord of all gentleness, Lord of all calm,
whose voice is contentment, whose presence is balm:
be there at our sleeping, and give us, we pray,
your peace in our hearts, Lord, at the end of the day.

Psalm 104.23
This setting was written to be a chorale in a Nativity tableau based on Luigi Santucci's *Wrestling with Christ*. Jan Struther's lovely text, and the need for it to be set afresh came after reading part of Santucci's evocation of Joseph: "…*a carpenter … Wood is sensitive and chaste and Joseph exercised his innocent sensuality by passing his open palms along planks smoothed by his carpenter's plane, by caressing the edges bevelled by his lathe, and breathing in his nostrils the fragrance of sawdust – that odour of hard work which, whenever anyone comes to the door, makes a man raise his sweaty brow knowing his visitor is a friend …*"

Jan Struther 1901-53

Doug Constable
© 1974/2021

SAWDUST 10 11 11 12

♩ = 88 Bluesey

Lord of all hopefulness, Lord of all joy, whose trust ever childlike no cares could destroy, be there at our waking, and give us, we pray, your bliss in our hearts, Lord,

Lord of all eagerness, Lord of all faith, whose strong hands were swift to be there at our labours, and give us, we pray, your strength in our hearts, Lord,

Lord of all kindliness, Lord of all grace, your hands swift to welcome, your arms to embrace, be there at our homing, and give us, we pray, your love in our hearts, Lord,

The accompaniment could be enhanced by the addition of a soft snare drum, and/or a guitar, and/or a solo instrument.

at the break of the day.
at the noon of the day.
at the eve of the day. *poco rit.*

♩ = 84   **poco rit.** ♩ = 80 Lord

Unacc.
Very calm
(ATB under Sops)   Lord of all

poco rit. Lord,

of all gent-le-ness, Lord of all calm, whose
gent-le-ness, Lord of all calm, Lord of all calm, whose
Lord of all calm,

voice is con-tent-ment, whose pre-sence is balm,
voice is con-tent-ment, whose pre-sence is balm,
whose pre - sence is balm,

be there at our sleeping, and
presence is balm, be there at sleeping, and
there

give us, we pray, your peace in our hearts, Lord,
give us, we pray, your peace in our hearts, Lord,

rit. *at the end of the day.*
at the end of the day, end of the day.

LOVE'S COMING

A cirrus-halo brushed her womb
and pricked, impulsed her inmost flesh
unspeakably. She bore love's holiness
in mortal time, made heaven a home.

Her child matured; chose homelessness;
became god-fellow to the poor in heart;
was constantly rejected. Yet love's art
in us still sows her womb afresh.

For us, wild cumuli and gales
announce the reaping Word, the Holy One,
whose quickening Love we fear. Thank God, the sun
renews all hope, while terror fails.

14.11.2015

53

Mary, weep not, weep no longer,
Now thy heart hath gained thy goal;
Here in truth the Gardener standeth,
But the Gardener of thy soul,
Who within thy spirit's garden
By his love hath made thee whole.

Now from grief and lamentation
Lift thy drooping heart with cheer;
While for love of him thou mournest,
Lo, thy Lord regained is here!
Fainting for him, thou hast found him;
All unknown, behold him near!

Love, who greets thee, lives unbounded,
Bids thee loose thy longing hold,
Sends thee to each sister, brother,
That the gospel might be told.
Tell whom thou hast seen and worshipped;
God's own Word shall make thee bold.

Now may all who hear your story
All be moved by your great love,
All be freed from fear and torment,
All give thanks to Christ above,
All inbreathe the Source of Glory,
All receive God's Spirit-Dove.

John 20.11-18
I wrote an arrangement of this hymn around 1975, from Plainsong Mode ii, for women's voices and piano. This combination of medieval and new words is here arranged for women's voices first, then SATB. A lightly beaten tambour could enhance the sense of this hymn as a dance.

Vv 1-2 Philippe de Grève 1236　　　　　　　　　　　　　　　　　　Doug Constable © 1996
[Trans. English Hymnal 1906]　　　　　　　　　　　　　　　　　　adapted from Mode ii
Vv 3-4 Doug Constable 1996

SILVER 87 87 87　　♩. = 100 Dancing

Freely

1. Mary, weep not, weep no longer,
Now thy heart hath gained its goal;
Here, in truth, the Gard'ner standeth,
But the Gard'ner of thy soul,
Who within thy spirit's garden
By his love hath made thee whole.

2. Now from grief and lamentation
Lift thy drooping heart with cheer;
While for love of him thou mournest,
Lo, thy Lord regained is here!
Weeping for him, thou hast found him;
All unknown, behold him near!

3. Love, who greets thee, lives unbounded,
Bids thee loose thy longing hold,
Sends thee to each sister, brother,
That the gospel might be told.
Tell whom thou hast seen and worshipp'd;
God's own word shall make thee bold!

4. Now may all who hear your story
All be moved by your great love,
All be freed from fear and torment,
All give thanks to God above,
All in-breathe the source of glory,
All receive God's Holy Dove.

54

Words and Music
Doug Constable
© 1981

PEARTREE 11 11 11 12

1. Most Holy Jesus, Thou way of truth and life,
almighty vanguard of vict-'ry in our strife:
bless us thy servants with peace from heaven above,
imprint our lives with thine own seal of selfless love.

Most holy Jesus, thou way of truth and life, almighty vanguard of victory in our strife:
bless us thy servants with peace from heaven above,
imprint our lives with thine own seal of selfless love.

As in the fullness of life restored, you came to free th'apostles from deadly fear and shame:
in sovereign freedom your presence still bestow
on us now gathered here for fellowship below.

And, as with mercy your wounded hands and side
you showed to Thomas – "My Lord and God!" he cried:
so grant us truly your nature to perceive, as we your sacred blood and body each receive.

Most glorious Saviour, the Father's only Son, enfleshed among us, to bind us into one:
breathe forth your Spirit, that, as we go our ways,
we may be bold to serve you all our livelong days.

And now, great Ruler of all our passing years accept our praises for all before who here
beheld your glory, who worshipped and adored,
who with their faithful lives declared you Christ and Lord.

By building surely on faith's foundation stone we hope to prosper, but for thy love alone;
that, when at last heaven and earth shall be no more,
thy name will hallowed be by all, thy face adored.

This hymn was written when I was Vicar of St Thomas' PEARTREE in Derby, to mark the centenary of the church's consecration on 21st December 1881.

Lord of life's journey, in faith and hope begun, whose love inspires us to do what must be done:
when for the last time we pass beyond this door, grant us to go the way that Christ has gone before.

Humbly we bless you for grace imparted here, for souls enlivened to love with holy fear;
in every word, every deed that bears your trace, people have seen you, human, godly, face to face.

Thanks for this building of wood and glass and stone,
your servant quarters, your temple, and your throne;
thanks for Saint Thomas, our patron and our guide:
awed by your glorious wounds, "My Lord and God!" he cried.

Lord of this body borne up by many a hand, Immortal Mercy, by whom frail mortals stand:
when mortar crumbles, and people fade away, clothe all of earth in heaven, in love's eternal day.

Our One Creator, Redeemer, Spirit, Friend, Source of time's river, life's estuary and end:
all we can offer is spread before Your gaze; as we depart, Lord, let us leave in peace and praise.

John 20.26-28   2 Corinthians 4.16-5.10   Luke 2.29
Thirty years after the parish of St Thomas celebrated the centenary of its foundation, the church was formally closed. Sung to the same music as the hymn written for the centenary service, these words were written to be the last act of the closing service. Happily, the building has now been re-purposed and internally re-built as a community hub, where the St Thomas Community still maintains Christian worship.

55

JEMYS HOP LM

Words and Music
Doug Constable
© 2002

1. Mysterious Lord of ev'ry dream, God's Spirit in the mind by night: shine in our heart's discernment's beam, teach us to pray for wisdom's light.

2. Let us perceive you in the flow of images that flood their own fate, us to ask the gifts to know your goodness, lest our hearts fall blind.

3. Teach us, with in this virtual world, where people build each good, not ill; find your riches here impearled, kingdom knocking at the gate.

4. Eternal seed and yeast, empower and nourish souls to wills each day, till tenderness, let none devour ev'n one of all saved by your will.

5. May Christ's own mind inform our sense, instruct and rule our all are saved at love's expense, and all are all spent in Christ's own way.

Mysterious Lord of every dream,
God's Spirit in the mind by night:
shine in our hearts discernment's beam,
teach us to pray for wisdom's light.

Let us perceive you in the flow
of images that flood the mind;
prompt us to ask the gifts to know
your goodness, lest our hearts fall blind.

Teach us, within this virtual world,
where people build each their own fate,
to find your riches here impearled,
heaven's kingdom knocking at the gate.

Eternal seed and yeast, empower
and nourish souls to good, not ill;
teach tenderness, let none devour
ev'n one of all saved by your will.

May Christ's own mind inform our sense,
instruct and rule our wills each day,
till all are saved at love's expense,
and all are spent in love's own way.

1 Kings 3.5-12 Matthew 13.31-33 and 44-46
Behind this hymn is the story of the Lord appearing to Solomon in a dream, commanding him to ask for whatever he wished. In this hymn we, like Solomon, ask for wisdom. The hymn is a kind of consecration of our unconscious life, acknowledging that images that may seem strange or outlandish in the everyday can, under the Holy Spirit's guidance, bring the mystery of God's presence to the light and direction of our consciousness.
The music was written while Jessica Mary was in Hospital.

56

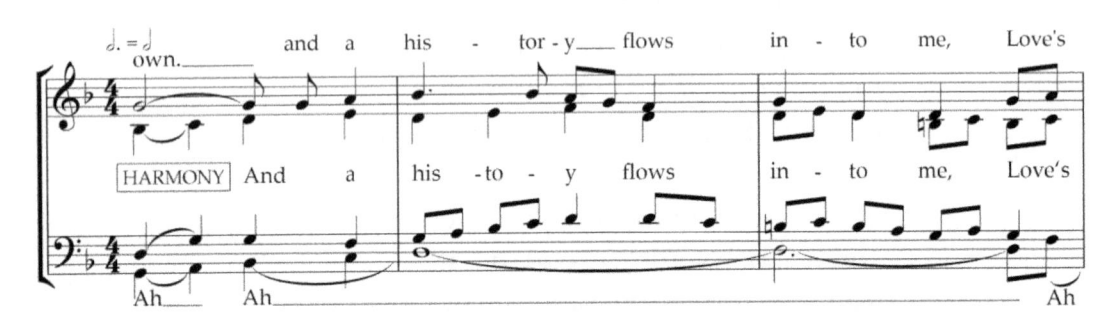

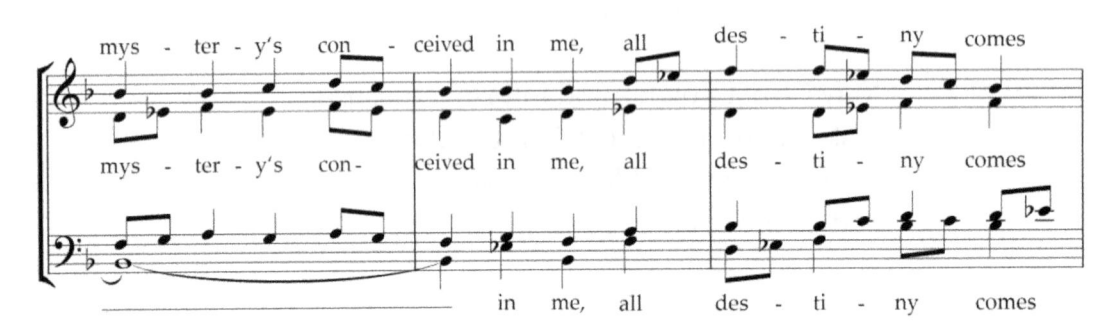

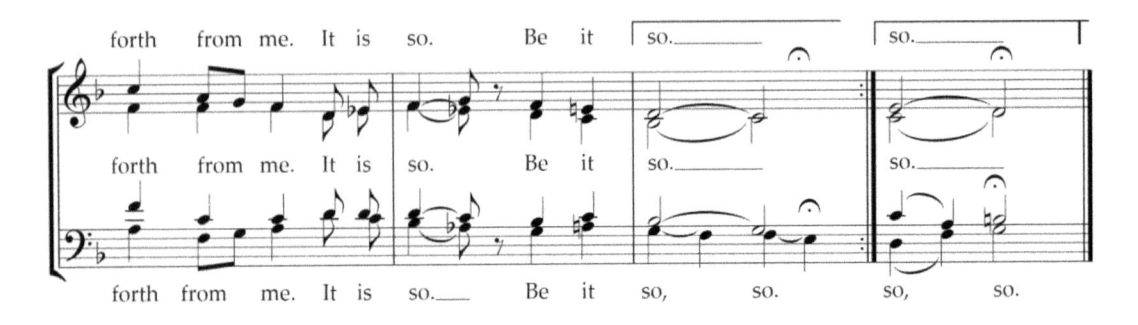

INTERGENERATION 11 11 11 11 9886

Words and Music:
Doug Constable
© 1996

♩. = 50 No one remembers my mother, my father, but I am their daughter, the fruit of their loins.

SOPS and ALTS, solo, semi-chorus, or full

I am the daughter of bliss and of blessing, whose hopes I inherit, whose prayers are my own.

♩. = ♩ and a history flows into me, Love's

HARMONY And a histo-y flows into me, Love's

Ah   Ah   Ah

mystery's conceived in me, all destiny comes

mystery's conceived in me, all destiny comes

in me, all destiny comes

forth from me. It is so. Be it so. so.

forth from me. It is so. Be it so. so.

forth from me. It is so. Be it so, so. so, so.

No one remembers my mother, my father,
but I am their daughter, the fruit of their loins;
I am the daughter of bliss and of blessing,
whose hopes I inherit, whose prayers are my own;
> *and a history flows into me,*
> *Love's mystery's conceived in me;*
> *all destiny comes forth from me;*
> *It is so. Be it so.*

No one remembers my childhood and growing,
yet I am a woman and child of my age;
I am a sister of male and of female,
whose hopes I embody, whose prayers are my own;
> *and a history &c*

Angels remember my time of awakening,
whence I am a mother, and child of my Lord;
I am beloved of earth and of heaven,
whose hopes I inspirit, whose prayers are my own.
> *and a history &c*

All will remember my first-born, my love-child,
the fruit of the promise to ages foretold;
he is the saviour embracing all history,
whose hopes I inhabit, whose prayers are my own.
> *and a history &c*

Please to remember your mothers, your fathers,
for you are their offspring, the fruit of their loins;
you are the bearers of bliss and of blessing:
our hopes you inherit; my prayers you may own.
> *Now all history flows on from me,*
> *Love's mystery's received from me,*
> *Love's destiny goes forth from me;*
> *it is so. Be it so.*

Written to celebrate the birthday of the Mother of Jesus Christ, these sentiments are a kind of extemporization on the themes of Annunciation and Magnificat.

57

Eric Milner-White 1884-1963
© 1994 Friends of York Minster

Doug Constable
© 1998

♩ = 84 Tenderly. Expressive

O Lord Jesus Christ, by thy tender power, impart to me thy lowliness; impart to me your purity; impart to me your strength of prayer; impart to me your love of the Father; impart to me your perfect priesthood, and your love of souls, O my Lord and God.

58

O Blessed Fire within, beyond
each kindled flesh, that burns
with life's desire for love's free bond,
for whom all being yearns:

we bless You for the leaping flame
that greets Your love come near,
the catching spark that speaks Your Name
through each embodied here.

Scorched by Your grace, we here confess
to lusting after love,
to grasping at Your gracious 'Yes',
Your self-gift from above.

Some lust, and claim it's nature's way
of feeling your embrace;
they do not wait to hear you say
love needs life's breathing space.

O Blessed Christ, burn up my will,
refine my inmost core;
re-kindle each soiled soul, until
we flame for evermore.

Rule all our thoughts, our every choice;
make all our senses glow;
then, by your grace, all will rejoice
in Love fleshed forth, here, now.

Matthew 5.27-28
This hymn attempts a response to Jesus' searching words. The music was written on the day researchers published the results of the Human GENOME project. Some might argue we are programmed to believe that lusting is indeed nature's way of feeling God's embrace. While this may appear an argumentative piece (one friend declared it "... a workshop!"), it is in fact a hymn of thanksgiving, contrition, and a prayer for love to be self-giving.

Words and Music:
Doug Constable
© 2001

GENOME CM

1. O Blessed Fire within, beyond each leaping flame that kindled flesh, that burns with life's desire for love's free bond, for whom all being burns:

2. We bless You for the here confess that greets your love come near, with the love, that speaks Your gracious Name 'Yes'. for each embodied here.

3. Scorched by Your grace, we lusting after love, to catching spark that grasping at Your self-gift from above.

tenuto

4. Some

lust, and claim it's nature's way of feeling Your embrace; they do not wait to hear You say: Love needs life's breathing space. 5. O

Blessed Christ, burn up my will, re- fine my inmost core; kindle each soiled soul, until we rejoice in flame forevermore. 6. Rule

all our thoughts, our ev'ry choice; make all our senses glow; then, by your grace, all Love fleshed forth, here, now.

59

Philip Doddrige (1702-51 altd DC)
NAOMOAB 86866
♩ = 96 Slow trudge

Doug Constable
© 1979

1. O God of Bethel, by whose hand thy people still are fed,
Who through this weary pilgrimage hast all our fathers and all our mothers led:

2. Our vows and prayers we here present before thy throne of grace;
God of our forebears, be the God of their succeeding race, of their succeeding race.

3. Through each perplexing path of life our wand'ring footsteps guide;
give us each day our daily bread, and raiment fit provide, and raiment fit provide.

4. O spread thy cov'ring wings around till all our striving cease,
and at our hearts' desired abode our souls arrive in peace, our souls arrive in peace.

An instrumental verse between sung verses 3 and 4 works well.

O God of Bethel, by whose hand
  thy people still are fed,
  who through this weary pilgrimage
  hast all our fathers
  and all our mothers led:

Our vows and prayers, we now present
  before thy throne of grace;
  God of our forebears, be the God
  of their succeeding race,
  of their succeeding race.

Through each perplexing path of life
  our wandering footsteps guide;
  give us each day our daily bread,
  and raiment fit provide,
  and raiment fit provide.

O spread thy covering wings around
  till all our strivings cease,
  and at our hearts' desired abode
  our souls arrive in peace,
  our souls arrive in peace.

Ruth 1.16-22; Psalm 107.4-7
This setting was composed for a musical presentation at Lee Abbey about the Book of Ruth. It evokes the weary journey to her home in Bethlehem of widowed Naomi, and of Ruth, her Moabite daughter-in-law, also a widow.

60

KETTLE 86 68

Words and Music
Doug Constable
© 2001

♩ = 100 Smoothly flowing

1. O Hidden Source of love, resource Yourself in thirsty souls; fill up these empty bowls with Spirit-grace for life's long course.

2. From Sinai into sin we've gone by way of loss and doubt; help us to turn about and drink from You, till grace be done.

3. We suffer, and endure, and hope, and are relieved by love; anointed from above, we choose again heaven's upward slope.

4. Refresh not only us, also the souls whose blood runs stale; that in you we are at Grail all may commune, and human grow.

5. O Christ, revealing God the Source sprung for the world to come: in you we are at home and drenched with love for life's long course.

O Hidden Source of love, resource
Yourself in thirsty souls;
fill up these empty bowls
with Spirit-grace for life's long course.

From Sinai into sin we've gone
by way of loss and doubt;
help us to turn about
and drink from You, till grace be done.

We suffer, and endure, and hope,
and are relieved by love;
anointed from above,
we choose again heaven's upward slope.

Refresh not only us, also
the souls whose blood runs stale;
that in the eternal Grail
all may commune, and human grow.

O Christ, revealing God the Source
sprung for the world to come:
in you we are at home
and drenched with love for life's long course.

Exodus 17.1-7; John 4.3-12; Romans 5.1-11
In essence, this hymn expounds the prayer of the Samaritan woman, *Sir, give me this water, that will become (in me) a spring...gushing up to eternal life*. As we sing, being ourselves spiritually thirsty, we identify with her, and with *the whole congregation of Israel* who *quarrelled with Moses*. In referring to 'the wilderness of Sin' (that is Sinai) verse 2 indulges a shameful but also helpful pun, for we are like those lost and doubting in the desert. 'The eternal Grail' in verse 4 refers to the medieval legend of the cup from which Jesus gave the wine that is his 'blood of the new covenant'.
The music was conceived in the Kenneth KETTLE Building of King Alfred's College (now the University of Winchester).

61

J.R.Peacey 1896-1971

Doug Constable
© 1973

PEACEYMOUTH 88 88 88
♩ = 104 Whole-line phrasing

O Lord, we long to see your face,
to know you risen from the grave.
But we have missed the joy and grace
of seeing you as others have.
Yet in your company we'll wait,
and we shall see you, soon or late.

O Lord, we long to see your face,
to know you risen from the grave,
but we have missed the joy and grace
of seeing you, as others have;
yet in your company we'll wait,
and we shall see you, soon or late.

O Lord, we do not know the way,
nor clearly see the path ahead,
so often, therefore, we delay
and doubt your power to raise the dead;
yet with you we will firmly stay,
you are the truth, the life, the way.

We find it hard, Lord, to believe;
all habit makes us want to prove:
we would with eye and hand perceive
the truth and person whom we love;
yet as in fellowship we meet,
you come yourself, each one to meet.

You come to us, our God, our Lord;
you do not show your hands and side;
but faith has its more blest reward;
in love's assurance we confide.
Now we believe, that we may know,
and in that knowledge daily grow.

John 20.24-29
A team of us from Lee Abbey took part in a Mission in the Parish of Holy Epiphany, Bournemouth. We offered a presentation that included a dramatized interpretation of St Thomas' experience of Christ's resurrection. This setting of PEACEY's words was written to be a part of that scene.

62

REMIGIUS 87 87

Words and Music
Doug Constable
© 2008

1. "O my people, sisters, brothers, all who breathe beneath the sun:
you were born to bond with others in the love that
makes us one, in the love that makes us one.

2. But, my people, fathers, mothers, see what want of love has done:
you've ig-nored, re-ject-ed others, mocked my prayer that
all be one, mocked my prayer that all be one.

3. Please, my people, come together in the life my death has won;
each with other, let me tether each to all, that
love may run, each to all, that love may run."

4. 'A-men' hearts and hands make answer, reaching out till all are one.
Heav'nly Source, Divine Enhancer, Love-with-us, Your
will be done, Love-with-us, Your will be done!

"O my people, sisters, brothers,
all who breathe beneath the sun:
you were born to bond with others
in the love that makes us one.

"But, my people, fathers, mothers,
see what want of love has done:
you've ignored, belittled, others,
mocked my prayer that all be one.

"Please, my people, come together
in the life my death has won;
each with other, let me tether
each to all, that love may run."

'Amen' hearts and hands make answer,
reaching out till all are one.
Heavenly Source, Divine Enhancer,
Love with us: Your will be done!

Micah 6.3-5 2; Corinthians 5-16-6.2; John 17.20-21
To help in preparations for the Lambeth Conference of 2008 hymns were asked for. This was my offering. The context of the conference was extremely painful; there were even fears that the Anglican Communion might break apart.
The shape of the text is based on texts that formed the liturgical Good Friday Reproaches from the Cross.

Mercredi Des Cendres
for Nathanaël

Three writers in the Bible tell
  of Jesus, who loved God so well
he got himself baptized, and then
    spent weeks with wild beasts in their den.

In deserts, where the wild beasts roam,
  most people do not feel at home;
no food to eat or drink, no bed
    with pillows to support their head.

In deserts people feel afraid,
  but heroes there are formed and made;
instead of killing beasts, they tend
    and tame them, make each one their friend.

For six weeks Jesus did not eat,
  he fainted in the noon-day heat;
but why he hungered, we should know:
    it was because he loved God so.

The Tempter came to him, and said
  "Command these stones to be made bread;
for you can do it, yes you can,
    since you're God's Son, not just a man."

"It's true," thought Jesus: "Yes, I could;
  but I will not be really good
unless I feed on every word
    that comes from out the mouth of God."

The cunning Tempter by and by
  led Jesus to a cliff-edge high,
and said "Although the drop be sheer,
    God's Son could safely jump from here."

"I know," thought Jesus: "I'm the one;
  but this poor Tempter's not much fun.
The law of gravity defy?
    Not I; for, if I do, I'll die."

The Tempter, then: "See, in my purse
  rich galaxies, the universe:
all will be yours, each land and sea,
    when you fall down and worship me."

Then Jesus growled! the Tempter's cry
  resounded far and wide. "Now I,"
said Jesus sternly, "I'll tell you
    what you and I are going to do.

"We're going to worship God alone,
    the God of love on heaven's great throne,
ev'n though you'd rather anything
    than bow before the Most High King.

"But do not be afraid, my friend,
  for love will find you in the end."
With that the Tempter slunk away;
    said, "I'll be back another day."

Now Jesus blessed our Father, God;
  and angels brought him spirit-food.
He took a rest, was filled with zest
    for partying; but lacked a guest.

"Hey you!" he called: "Come here, and feast,
  all from the north, south, west, and east."
And one by one, through life's long Lent,
    they shared that food, as Jesus meant.

2015

63

O Thou, beyond all culture, creed, and caste,
Eternal Being, always First and Last,
Perennial Mystery to each and all,
at home in every heart, to hand, on call:

Dear Holy Other, Father, Mother, Friend,
Companion of all living, without end,
to You, in whom all being comes to be,
I sing my thanks for life embracing me;

thanks for my part in all creation knows:
this earth is shared with strangers, friends, and foes;
of one blood, nations, neighbours, with one mind
desire that all be well, all humans, kind.

Alas! – I know, I'm selfish to the core,
I hoard more than my share of common store.
Help me to turn back home, and find You there,
welcoming the humble to our common fare.

Spirit of common wealth, to You we pray:
help us to love in truth throughout life's day;
may we, Your common people, never cease
to set Your joy before us, making peace.

Words: Doug Constable © 2021
Music: FARLEY CASTLE
Henry Lawes 1596-1662
Metre: 10 10 10 10

Acts 2.43-47a, 4.33-35

This prayer is based in the belief that being converted to God necessarily entails becoming converted to one's neighbour. That in turn means acknowledging that we belong in the community of creation, that we owe loyalty to global society before individual self-interest.

64

VEXILLA NOVA LM

Words and Music
based on Mode i
Doug Constable
© 2001

♩ = 92

1. O Thou the Breath, the Light of all, the Driving Power of Life: you call our dried up selves to bloom again, to rise full-bodied, like new grain.
2. Our peoples from your cov'nant stray, with no sure guide, each their own way; the story of Christ's love and cross is scarcely known, great loss.
3. And we have stories to confess: how with the cross Christ's stubborn folk oppress the vuln'er'ble, some times choosers, death, who pro-test with their ev'ry breath.
4. Can they, can we, sick dry bones live? Can wounded, stubborn souls forgive? Can self-declared free crack of doom; so truth where in all from the grow?
5. O Thou the Breath, the Light of all: with you we stand; without we fall. Your voice can mend the crack of doom; so call us, praising, tomb.

O Thou the Breath, the Light of all,
the Driving-Power of Life: you call
our dried-up selves to bloom again,
to rise full-bodied, like new grain.

Our peoples from your covenant stray,
with no sure guide, each their own way;
the story of Christ's love and cross
is scarcely known, though great the loss.

And we have stories to confess:
how with the cross Christ's folk oppress
the vulnerable, sometimes to death;
who protest with their every breath.

Can they, can we, sick, dry bones, live?
Can wounded, stubborn souls forgive?
Can self-declared free-choosers know
self-humbling, by which all may grow?

O Thou the Breath, the Light of all:
with You we stand; without we fall.
Your voice can mend the crack of doom;
so call us, praising, from this tomb.

Genesis 9.8-17; Ezekiel 37.1-14; John 11.1-45
Written for Passion Sunday, the music of this hymn – VEXILLA NOVA - intentionally echoes the start of the great hymn of this day 'The royal banners forward go' to the plainsong 'Vexilla Regis'. Two stories provide the background: the valley of the dry bones, and the raising of Lazarus. The opening line quotes Neil Douglas-Klotz' translation of 'The Lord's Prayer' in Aramaic. Verse 2 refers to God's covenant with all creation, articulated in Christian understanding through the ministry, death and resurrection of Jesus. In Europe this was once deeply inscribed in popular culture, but evidence suggests this is no longer the case.
In verse 4 "self-declared free-choosers" are those – perhaps us - who choose to consume religious experience rather than fulfil the demands of religious calling.

65

O Thou, who came to serve,
to seek the lost, and save:
our ransom, Human One, you gave
your life, that all might live.

You pray for us: we crave
security and love;
we fall, but on the cross you move
Our Father to forgive.

The love of God you prove
in raising us above
each mortal's need for self to thrive:
yourself our humble slave.

Jesus, we will be brave
to bear our cross, and strive
to follow where you lead, and live
to serve, to seek, to love.

Redeemer, Holy Dove,
Creator God: receive
the ransomed world's best thanks, and weave
a new world from the grave.

Words: Doug Constable © 2018
Music: ST GEORGE
H.J.Gauntlett 1805-76
Metre: CM

Mark 10.45
'The Son of Man came not to be served but to serve and give his life a ransom for many.'

66

One dark night transcendent light flooded our hearts with peace and pardon.

This bright day we, blossoming, say, Our lives are like a watered garden.

Evermore shall praises soar, for love has come to share our burden.

Gloria! Hallelujah! Jubilate! Exultate!

Day and night this heavenly light leads us all to holy freedom.

Jeremiah 31.12
This unusual hymn, a kind of rhapsody for all seasons, may look complicated, but it is nearly all based on a pattern of call and response. As such, what looks like a choir anthem affords the possibility of a rich dialogue between choir and congregation. A leader or leaders teach a line and everyone sings it straight after them. The piece is so written that, wherever it may seem complicated, singers can take the line of least resistance, without weakening the whole. But it can also be developed into something more elaborate, as singers may wish.

WATER GARDEN

Words amd Music
Doug Constable
© 1996

♩ = 100 Not hurried

One dark night transcendent light flooded our hearts with peace and pardon.

This bright day we blossoming say, Our lives are like a watered garden.

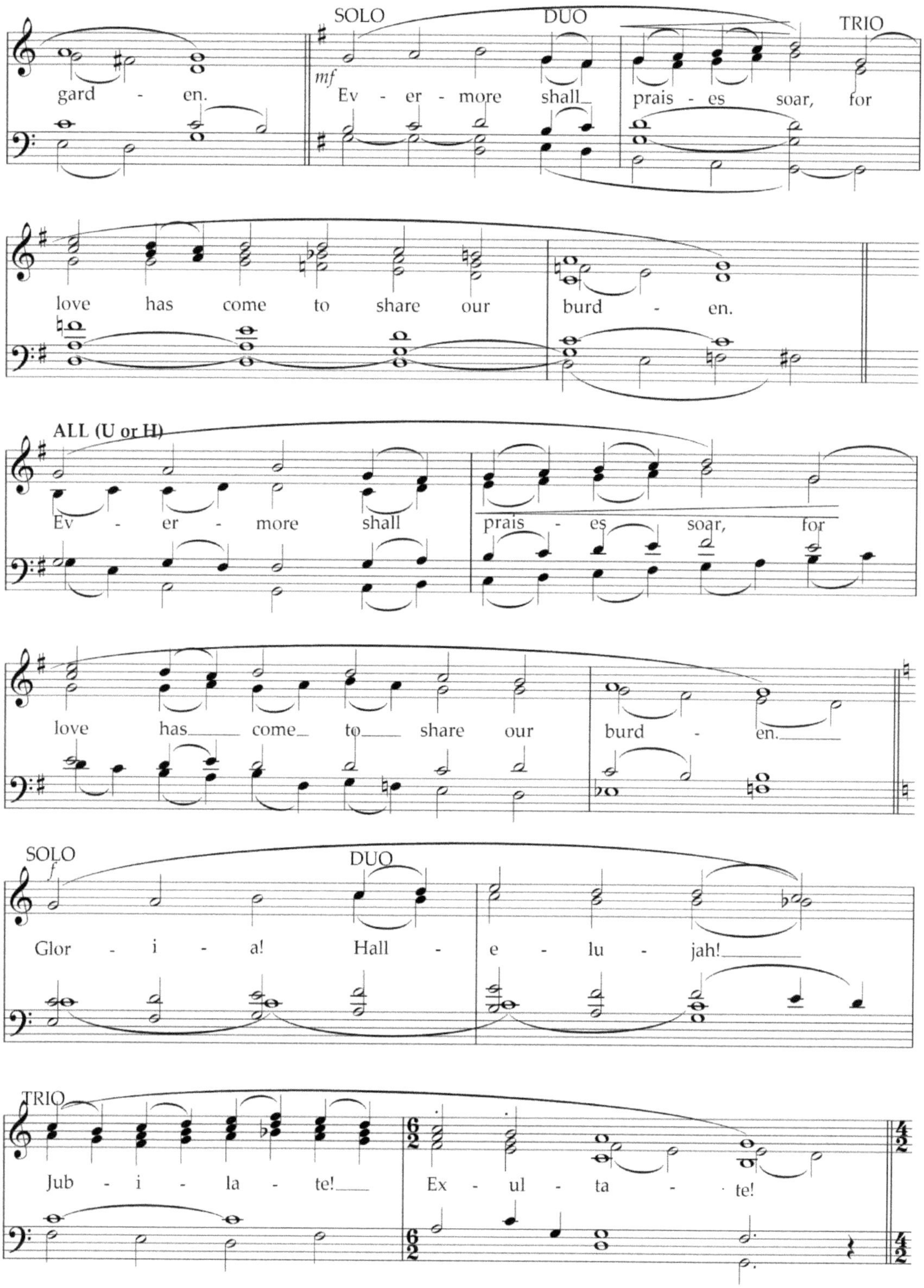
SOLO
DUO
TRIO
mf
gard - en. Ev - er - more shall_ prais - es soar, for
love has come to share our burd - en.
ALL (U or H)
Ev - er - more shall prais - es soar, for
love has__ come__ to__ share our burd - en.__
SOLO
f
DUO
Glor - i - a! Hall - e - lu - jah!__
TRIO
Jub - i - la - te!__ Ex - ul - ta - te!

ALL (U or H)
Glor - i - a! Hall - e- lu - jah!
Jub - i - la - te! -
-Ex - ul - ta - te!
Acc.
SOLO
DUO
TRIO
Day and night this holy - y light leads love's way to life in free - dom.
ALL (Unison)
Day and night this hol - y light floods us like a
simile
wat ered gard- en, leads us all to hol - y
rall.
free - dom!
HARMONY
Acc.

On fearing and not fearing
And unto man he saith, Behold the fear of the Lord, that is wisdom, and to depart from evil is understanding. (Job 28.28)

Dear Love, whose heat condenses from above
in drops that warmly drench all loves on earth,
and intimates that life will lovely prove
when people honour You, and own Your worth:
no speech or language can define Your Name,
nor any praise encompass all Your Throne;
such as they are, our prayer-deeds all catch flame
by action of Your grace, Your grace alone.
When once, in time, You came from far beyond
conceiving, quickened as embodied soul,
and called on all the world to turn, respond
with mercy, mend each un-loved heart till whole,
You led, Lord Christ, strange friends from far and near
home to Your heaven, evaporating fear …

A whisper, 'fear' … and nerves are set on edge;
to think we harbour fear stirs up deep rage:
"We need no god to cast out fear, to dredge
our memories' depths. We dis-engage
ourselves from such unhelpful words as 'cross',
'deny yourself', 'touch not', and 'God alone';
we don't accept that people suffer loss
when they disown religion, who need none."

Ah, Lord, You are abused, and silently
endure in grief our sad, disordered way;
upon Your cross-shaped throne (could we but see)
You draw us to Yourself, while all betray
the Love that guides and heals and makes us good,
and always at the cost of love's heart-blood.

The thing is this: when God says 'Thou shalt not …',
divine authority works dignity –
dynamic safety – in those Love-begot
who guard the tender shoots of liberty.
The source and ground of every good and ill
cannot be contra-facted, though our pride
be certainly offended; but yet, still
above us, and within, they over-ride –
these angels – softly intimating care
for all, for every truth that comes to birth.

And there is only one way forward: to bear
the will's humiliation, kiss the earth,
submit to One who slays us and upraises
to the depths, whence wisdom Love-ward praises.

13.12.2020

67

MORLEY 87 87

Words and Music
Doug Constable
© 1996/2007

1. Out of the ground we hear the cry that
calls to You, our Father, the
cry of blood that's shed today
for many a sister, brother.

2. Silent the sound of some who die in-
sulted or rejected; they
dies from want of love today,
love turned cold, demented.

3. Curses abound from some who die struck
down and unlamented; they
lie like monuments today
to our own terrors gather.

4. Out of the ground we hear their sigh who
hoped in you, our Father, their
sigh that doubts you hear today,
while all our sisters, brothers.

5. You are the ground in which we die and
rise, for love of others; in
You we hope to live today
for the gift of heav'n for sharing.

6. Into our hearts come thoughts of pain, for
death seems overpow'ring; and
love reborn goes forth again,
the gift of heav'n for sharing.

Out of the ground we hear the cry
that calls to you, our Father:
the cry of blood that's shed today
of many a sister, brother.

Silent the sound of some who die
insulted or rejected;
they die from want of love today,
by bitter pains infected.

Curses abound from some who die
struck down and unlamented;
they lie like monuments today
to love turned cold, demented.

Out of the ground we hear their sigh
who hoped in you, our Father -
their sigh that doubts you hear today,
while our own terrors gather.

You are the ground in whom we die
and rise, for love of others;
in You we hope to live today
for all our sisters, brothers.

Into our hearts come thoughts of pain,
for death seems overpowering;
and love re-born goes forth today,
the gift of heaven for sharing.

Genesis 4.1-16
This hymn is a meditation on the story of Cain and Abel. The tune is called MORLEY in homage to Thomas Morley (1557-c1603), the opening of whose Verse Anthem *Out of the deep have I called to thee, O Lord* this hymn faintly echoes.

68

Henry Francis Lyte (1793-1847)
LEESON 87 87 87
♩ = 142 Flowing whole lines

Doug Constable
© 1976/97

1. Praise my soul, the King of heaven;
To his feet thy tribute bring.
Ransomed, healed, restored, forgiven,
Who like me his praise should sing?
Alleluya! Praise him! Praise him!
Alleluya! Praise him! Praise him!
Praise the everlasting King.

2. Praise him for his grace and favour To our fathers in distress; Praise him still the same as ever, Slow to chide and swift to bless. Alleluya! Praise him! Praise him! Alleluya! Praise him! Praise him! Glorious in his faithfulness.

♩ = 132 HARMONY
mp 3. Father-like, he tends and spares us; Well our feeble frame he
mp unacc.

knows, In his hands he gent - ly bears us, Res - cues
♩ = 136
us from all our foes. acc. Al - le - lu - ya! acc. Praise him!
Praise him! acc. Al - le - lu - ya! acc. Praise him! Praise him! Wide - ly as his
DESCANT Ang - els help us to a -
UNISON 4. Ang - els help us to a -
♩ = 142
mer - cy flows.
dore him; Ye be - hold him face to face;
dore him; Ye be - hold him face to face;
Sun and moon bow down be - fore him, Dwell - ers all in
Sun and moon, bow down be - fore him, Dwell - ers all in

This setting (without descant) was composed to be sung (in unison) at a Lee Abbey re-union in Bristol, led by Rodney LEESON; and the tune is dedicated to his memory. The more elaborate arrangement here is provided for those who would like it. Normally, the accompaniment to the first verse will suffice for the whole hymn.

69

Scottish Psalter 1650
Doug Constable
© 1993

ORATE CM

♩ = 84 Steady pulse. Quiet, expressive.

1. Pray that Jerusalem may have peace and felicity: let them that love thee and thy palaces have still prosperity.
2. Therefore I wish that peace may still within thy walls remain, and ever may thy palaces God our Lord have still prosperity.
3. Now, for my friends' and brethren's sake, "Peace be in thee" I'll say; and for the house of God our Lord I'll seek thy peace alway.

D.C.

Psalm 122.6-9

As a boy, I warmed to the simple beauty of YORK, the 1615 Scottish setting to which this versification of part of Psalm 122 is usually sung. But as an adult I feel the need for something else as well: acknowledgement of the contested status of Jerusalem and the poignant atmosphere that needs must inflect all prayer for that holy city.

Salem Stones: a homily
Luke 19.41-44

Here's a little gospel poem
made especially for you,
all about how we can show 'em
Jesus Christ makes all things new.

If you go to Jeru*sal*em,
if you ever go one day,
you will see where stones have fallen,
after Jesus passed that way.

Once, these proud stones all surrounded
God's own city, full of song;
now, forlorn, they lie there, grounded.
Is that right, or is it wrong?

One brave lass said, "We should share it,
we should share our city fair."
One brave lad: "I cannot bear it;
I don't want those wreckers here:

"they're our enemies, they hate us,
they just want to break us down.
We should fight, lest they defeat us,
lest they drive us out of town."

Then the girl said, "Jesus taught us
to bless all our enemies;
we should pray for persecutors,
and forgive them , if you please."

"You're a softie, much too tender:
you don't want to face the pain.
Hard we must be. No surrender!
Mercy none – so will we gain!"

Like a gem she shone, but kinder:
"God commands us not to kill.
You should be a peace-defender:
fight with love; be patient still.

"Use your strength, and aim to live them –
these, the words of Jesus, who
while they nailed him, prayed, Forgive them,
for they know not what they do."

But the lad got higher, mightier,
stuck a piece of sticky tape
on the lassie's mouth, to quiet her;
boy behaving worse than ape.

Jesus saw it. Jesus wept then,
wept for all who mock his way:
"Peace you should have made; and kept them –
all my words – in this your day.

"You would then see here is God come,
helping enemies be friends.
But you'd rather not see; so doom
fells your walls, your stones upends."

Both dear brave ape and brave dear gem:
how God loves them to the end!
Stretched upon the cross to save them,
Jesus shows them how to mend

all their broken walls and faces,
take each other to their heart;
cross-shaped love always displaces
fear, and gives each one a part

in sounding heaven's songs of new earth:
Living stones stand up and shout;
open doors bid, 'Come to our hearth;
sinners here turn inside out.'

So hear this, and when you've heard it,
sing it, if you will, with me.
Short and simple, once you've purred it,
you can pray it openly:

Let there be peace on the earth,
and let it begin with me,
for peace is Christ on the earth –
may Jesus be seen in me.

7 March 2010
for a Family Eucharist

70

REDOULINE CM
♩ = 96

Words and Music:
Doug Constable
© 1996

1. Revitalise our spirits, Lord, revive our zest for life, Enthuse us with your boundless joy, intensify our love!
2. For weariness afflicts us, Lord, dull habits know no end; and, though we mean to change our ways, to hopelessness we tend.
3. We hear that you will come again to judge both live and dead; not to condemn faint hearts, or false: to save the world instead.
4. Poor anxious souls ask, Tell us when. Says fearfulness, Too soon. Are you so dreadful, so unkind? Do you intend our doom?

Revitalise our spirits, Lord,
revive our zest for life,
enthuse us with your boundless joy,
intensify our love!

For weariness afflicts us, Lord,
dull habits know no end;
and, though we mean to change our ways,
to hopelessness we tend.

We hear that you will come again
to judge both live and dead;
not to condemn faint hearts, or false:
to save the world instead.

Poor anxious souls ask, *Tell us when.*
Says fearfulness, *Too soon.*
Are you so dreadful, so unkind,
do you intend our doom?

The news that cheers says, You are Love:
you heal all grief and shame,
restoring strength to burdened hearts,
dissolving memory's blame.

Eternal Now, our Source, our End:
raise up your power this day;
come, grace our lives with love renewed;
God's zest let all display!

Romans 13.11-14 and Matthew 24.36-44.
A hymn for any day of the year, but especially Advent Sunday.
The music was conceived while visiting friends at their home REDOULINE in the Dordogne.

71

Soul of creation, soul of life,
in whom both seed and fruit are rife
with joy that feeds the human soul,
with good that makes the wounded whole:

humbly, before the close of day,
we ask that truth light up our way;
as we put off our world-worn face,
cleanse and restore us by Your grace.

Now, by the Holy Spirit's light,
reveal such wrongs as we can right,
quieten our minds, set us at peace,
let generous love through each increase.

Help us attend to here and now,
all You have given with thanks avow;
help us to offer all our fears:
Saviour, redeem our faithless years.

Help us to own all that's done well,
help us to see love's harvest swell;
where we fall short, free us from shame:
renew with hope, in vision's flame.

Then we, with countless pilgrims blessed,
praising, will face our welcome guest:
Heaven-incarnate here on earth,
God, find a home at our poor hearth.

Soul of the new creation, seal
such love in each that all may heal;
may we, with Christ before our eyes,
fulfil our lives, to glory rise.

Words: Doug Constable © 2018
Music: HURSLEY
Katholischer Gesangbuch c.1774 Vienna
Metre: LM

These words came after 'bathing' in *Sun of my soul, thou Saviour dear,* the lovely evening hymn of John Keble 1792-1866.

72

Send us out in the power of thy Spirit
to live and work to thy praise and glory ...

Welcome the day, welcome its dawning!
Welcome the way, welcome its warning!
Welcome the new life! Welcome the bread of heaven!
Welcome the Lord who is broken and risen for joy, my friends,
                                  for joy, my friends,
                                  for joy my friends!

Christ is alive, life is elected!
Love will survive, love resurrected!
Rising together, raised by the wind of heaven,
welcome our interconnecting and flaming with joy, my friends,
                                  with joy, my friends,
                                  with joy, my friends!

Praise to our God! Praise to the Father!
Praise to the Son, praise to our brother!
Praise to the Spirit! Praise to the Three-in-One!
Praise to the sum of creation, salvation, and joy, my friends,
                                  and joy, my friends,
                                  and joy, my friends!

Acts 2.1

After a week in which the Lee Abbey Community and guests had been celebrating the ministry of the Holy Spirit, this hymn was written to close the Eucharist for Pentecost Sunday. Close on two hundred worshippers gathered in the Octagonal Lounge, so that the accompanying grand piano had to be played in the adjacent RED CORRIDOR.

69 Wel - come its warn - ing! Wel - come the new life!
love___ re - sur - rect - ed! Ris - ing to - geth - er,
Praise___ to our broth - er! Praise___ to the Spir - it!

77 Wel - come the Bread of Heaven! Wel - come the Lord who is brok - en and ris - en for
raised___ by the wind of heaven, wel - come our int - er - con - nect - ing and flam - ing with
Praise___ to the Three - in - One! Praise to the God of sal - va - tion and laught - er and

85 joy, my friends! for joy, my friends! for joy, my [1.2. friends!___
joy, my friends, with joy, my friends, with joy, my friends!___
joy my friends! and life, my friends! and life, my

91 *cresc...*

95 friends!___

171

73

SCHUTZ 7776

Words and Music
Doug Constable
© 1996

1. Shall the wolf live with the lamb?
   leopard lie down with the kid?
   by a little child be led?
   Some may always doubt it.

2. Shall the cow graze with the bear?
   ox eat straw beside the lion?
   child play on the viper's den?
   Some may always doubt it.

3. Shall the Jew sup with the Goy?
   Arab with Israeli drink?
   for each other's young give thanks?
   Some may always doubt it.

4. Ulster Prod and Irish Taig?
   Sunni, Shia share their lands?
   neighbours grow in friendship's bonds?
   Some may always doubt it.

5. Branch of Jesse, Judge inspired,
   fired by love and fear of God,
   Christ, you've slaked our thirst for blood.
   None need ever doubt it.

6. Trusting, childlike, chastened, we
   all would bear repentance' fruit:
   no more to destroy and hurt.
   Tell the world about it,

Shall the wolf live with the lamb? leopard lie down with the kid?
by a little child be led? Some may always doubt it.

Shall the cow graze with the bear? ox eat straw beside the lion?
child play on the viper's den? Some may always doubt it.

Shall the Jew sup with the Goy? Arab with Israeli drink?
for each other's young give thanks? Some may always doubt it.

Ulster Prod and Irish Taig? Sunni, Shia share their lands?
neighbours grow in friendship's bond? Some may always doubt it.

LGBs and straights be friends? loving as one chosen race?
find you in each other's face? Some may always doubt it.

Branch of Jesse, Judge Inspired, fired by love and fear of God,
Christ, you've slaked our thirst for blood. None need ever doubt it.

Trusting, childlike, chastened, we all would bear repentance' fruit:
no more to destroy and hurt. Tell the world about it.

Isaiah 11.1-10
This hymn reflects sceptically on Isaiah's great vision of peace, agreeing with Sportin' Life in *Porgy and Bess* that "It ain't necessarily so". Explicit topical references in hymns are rare, not least because circumstances change, making such references soon out of date. But some painfully topical references seem as if written into the enduring fabric of life; they need to be named in prayer.
While composing this hymn I had been listening to music by Heinrich Schütz, and the German word SCHUTZ - 'protection' – came to mind, because of the strength believers find in meditating on Christ crucified, who by his self-offering – if we will allow it – *slaked our thirst for blood.*

74

GWENDOLEN 777

Words and Music
Doug Constable
© 2002

1. Sov'reign of each unfolding hour by love enseeded,
sprung to flower for joyful fruiting forth in power:
'No, not so!' Lord, free us from deceit and woe.

2. living within your reign of peace is all we want, till
sin shall cease and ev'ry pris'ner find release.
set his fire against cheap peace that all desire.

3. Many claim your authority, presume to state what
truth must be; but rarely do their words agree.
give you praise. So may we serve you all our days.

4. Help us discern the way to go, though all the world cry,

5. Here we acclaim brave Jeremiah, who bore your yoke, and

6. Humble us, that we change our ways and welcome all who

Sovereign of each unfolding hour
by love en-seeded, sprung to flower
for joy full-fruiting forth in power:

living within your reign of peace
is all we want, till sin shall cease,
and every prisoner find release.

Many claim your authority,
presume to state what truth must be;
but rarely do their words agree.

Help us discern the way to go,
though all the world cry No, not so!
and set us free from fear of woe.

Let us acclaim brave Jeremiah,
who bore your yoke, and set his fire
against cheap peace that all desire.

Humble us, that we change our ways
and welcome all who give you praise,
and thrive before you all our days.

Jeremiah 27 and 28, specifically in 28.5-9
If Jeremiah featured in the Christian Calendar of Saints, this hymn could be sung on his feast-day. God commanded the prophet to make a yoke, put it on his neck, and order the king of Judah to put his and his people's necks *under the yoke of the king of Babylon*. Not surprisingly, the truth of Jeremiah's prophecy was challenged by an official establishment prophet.
In our age facing up to inconvenient and unpalatable truths remains a spiritual challenge.

75

Star-guided pilgrims come to find a king;
the fullness of humanity they bring:
gold shows their power, frankincense thirst for heaven,
myrrh speaks for mortals, 'May we be forgiven'.

They seek him first in corridors of power;
they find him nursed in lowly stable-bower:
with joy they lay their treasures at his feet,
and ponder life and death, that in him meet.

Here points the sword to pierce each mother's soul;
here speaks the Word of peace to all, 'Be whole';
here lies the infant Christ, God's self made strange;
here moves the love that moves the world to change.

Made wise, they go home by another way,
their lives enlightened by each heart's new day;
their old beliefs, that courted death by fear,
they now renounce, to live in holy cheer.

Dear Cosmic Mystery, by love made known,
Star-in-all-history, Love's Lowly Throne:
help us, who long for peace, to prize each trace
by which we find your future for our race.

Words: Doug Constable © 2013
Music: FARLEY CASTLE
Henry Lawes 1596-1662

Matthew 2.1-11
These words reflect on the 'Journey of the Magi, hoping to enfold us all now in what was revealed to them then.

76

Words and Music:
Doug Constable
© 1997

TEMPLEHOWTHOM 777 777 6

1. Like a sheep to slaughter led,
victim to the lions fed,
silent, you endured your dread:
Lamb of God, may ev'ry soul
brave their sentence, face their goal;
may we see the world made whole,
Saviour, Christ crucified,
Saviour, Christ crucified.

Jesus is condemned to death
Like a sheep to slaughter led,
victim to the lions fed,
silently enduring dread:
Lamb of God, may every soul
brave their sentence, face their goal;
may we see the world made whole…
    Saviour, Christ crucified.

Jesus receives the cross
Cursed, you bore the world's disgrace,
wore the shame of all our race,
suffered in each sinner's place:
go with all who bear their load,
yoke us each upon the road;
love, our all-sufficient goad…
    Saviour, Christ crucified.

Jesus falls for the first time
Christ our rock and our defence,
overwhelmed by violence,
one with suffering innocents:
when we, stumbling, grieve and sigh,
when, afflicted, crushed, we cry,
you will fall to lift us high…
    Saviour, Christ crucified.

Jesus is met by his mother
Son of love and lord of life,
sword of truth and cause of strife,
earth's full fruit, and heaven's
                  midwife:
we would worship, love, obey
God alone, that so we may
honour all who bear your way…
    Saviour, Christ crucified

The cross is laid on Simon of Cyrene
Brother of each hidden man,
shared with all the human clan,
glad of every helping hand:
though we feel reluctant, scared,
all unable, and impaired,
find us daring to have cared…
    Saviour, Christ crucified.

Veronica wipes the face of Jesus
Torn by thorns, and wreathed in pain,
yours the image that remains
when our God with blood is stained.
Women, men, with tenderness,
all: in everyone confess
Christ, the holy face we bless…
    Saviour, Christ crucified.

Jesus falls for the second time
Though you fall, your way is sure:
to fulfil, you will endure
all that law and love require.
When we lose love's chosen way,
let us not despair or stray;
God, with joy, come, crown that day…
    Saviour, Christ crucified.

Women of Jerusalem mourn for the Lord
You refuse our pity's tears;
we excuse our ruling fears -
pain confusing grief with care.
As we turn into the storm,
braving loss, oppression, harm,
be beside us, love's true form…
    Saviour, Christ crucified.

Jesus falls for the third time
No one knows the hell you knew,
none can tell what you went through
till you cried your last adieu.
When the light of life is gone,
faith and hope and love forlorn,
bring us to the Father's throne…
    Saviour, Christ crucified.

Jesus is stripped of his garments
In the flesh, and to the end
naked love will not pretend;
thus your life you recommend.
Grant us, in the midst of shame,
joy of love, embodied flame.
All your humble pride we claim…
    Saviour, Christ crucified.

Jesus is nailed to the cross
Does it have to happen thus:
captive nailed upon a cross?
Must we force our pound of flesh?
Though these mindless wounds appal,
by your prayer 'Forgive them all',
force is broken, love will heal…
    Saviour, Christ crucified.

Jesus dies on the cross
Love poured out, the heart is stilled:
heaven is earth-through-you-distilled,
all accomplished as God willed.
In your end is where we start,
you have won our thankful hearts:
life the gift your death imparts…
    Saviour, Christ crucified.

The body of Jesus is taken from the cross
Lord deceased, gone to the void,
body broken, seed destroyed,
drained into the ground of God:
dazed by absence of your breath,
crazed by memories of your death,
razed to silence, still we bless
    Saviour, Christ crucified.

The body of Jesus is laid in the tomb
Who could know that from the tomb
God would re-create a womb
to confound the priests of doom?
Into silence, into peace
we would go, till love release
all our joy, your life and grace…
    Saviour, Christ crucified.

The Stations of the Cross is a form of devotion that originated with fourth century pilgrims, who would retrace Jesus' journey from Pilate's house to Golgotha. The traditional form of the fourteen depictions of the Passion was established in the nineteenth century. It is a journey of imaginative recollection and prayer.
These fourteen prayers (all sung to the same music) were composed for Holy Week 1997 in Southampton City Centre Anglican Parish. The music was composed the day Dorothy Howell-Thomas came to lunch; she had been Archbishop William TEMPLE's secretary.

SING OUT, MY SOUL
for Tabitha

It starts down there
beneath the ground
that bears the weight
of joy, from where
the welcome sound
soars upward. Heart
to heart sings round,
blessing the air.
Each hand takes part,
till all are found
daring to share,
each one, their art.
It starts down here,
and with one bound
vaults heaven's gate:

love's opened throat.

15 October 2010

77

Summoned by your call, and gathered in your name,
answering disciples pray: Spirit of Jesus, come.

Gathered in your name, and waiting your good time,
patiently, disciples pray: Spirit of Jesus, come.

Waiting your good time, and sharing bread and wine,
faithfully disciples pray: Spirit of Jesus, come.

Sharing bread and wine, and bonded by your love,
gladly your disciples pray: Spirit of Jesus, come.

>Suddenly, descending,
>rush of wind and flame;
>all inspired, disciples say:
>Spirit of Christ, welcome!
>
>Suddenly, the church breaks
>forth in every tongue;
>now with *hwyl* apostles say:
>Spirit of Christ, well come!
>
>Now is saving grace to
>young and old proclaimed;
>endlessly God's people say:
>Spirit of Christ is come!
>
>Summoned to be one, and
>gathered in your name,
>joyfully today, we pray:
>Spirit of Christ, lead on!

Acts of the Apostles chapter 2
Outlining the story beginning "When the day of Pentecost had fully come." this hymn was written while my wife was visiting her parents in PENARTH.
Hwyl (hooil) is 'uplift', 'cheer', 'joy'. A Welsh word, it's what may happen when the singing or the preaching 'takes off'.

PENARTH 65 76

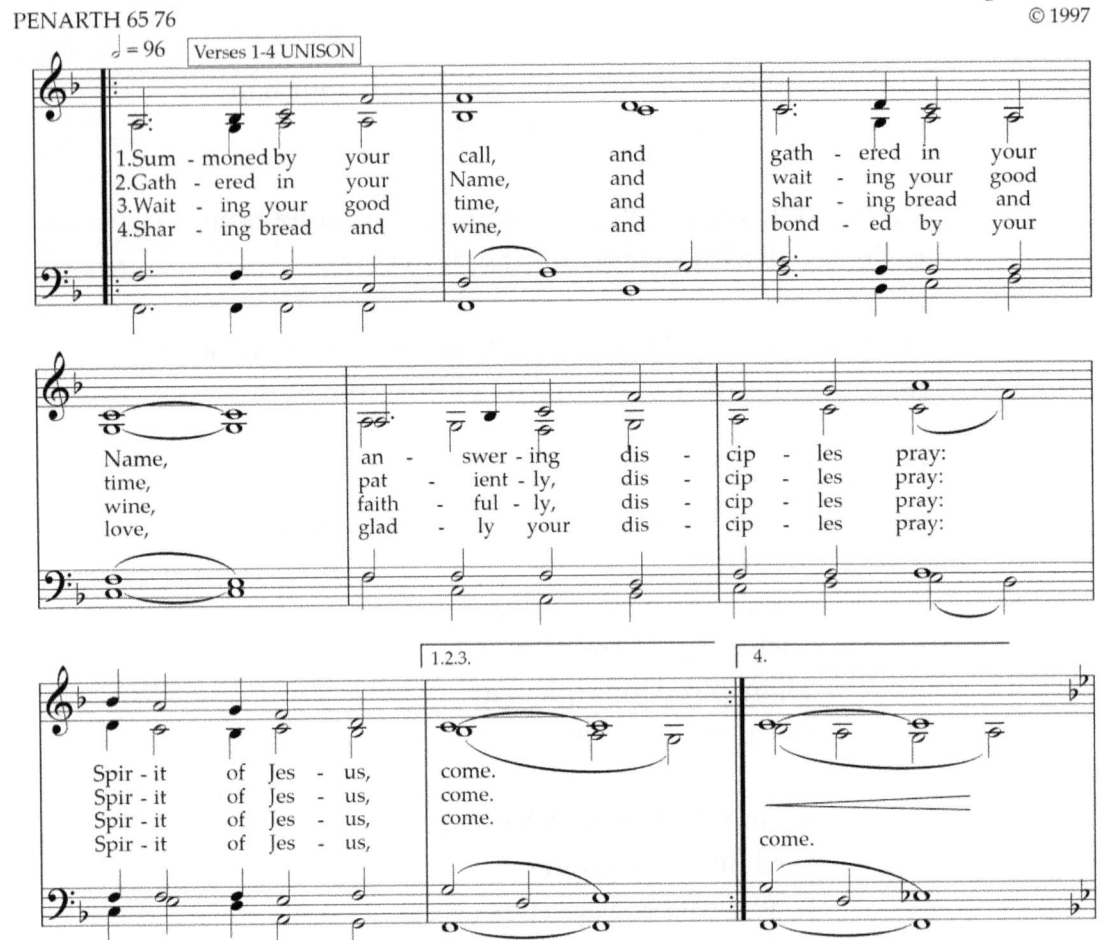

Words and Music:
Doug Constable
© 1997

♩ = 96 — Verses 1-4 UNISON

1. Summoned by your call, and gathered in your Name, answering disciples pray: Spirit of Jesus, come.
2. Gathered in your Name, and waiting your good time, patiently, disciples pray: Spirit of Jesus, come.
3. Waiting your good time, and sharing bread and wine, faithfully, disciples pray: Spirit of Jesus, come.
4. Sharing bread and wine, and bonded by your love, gladly your disciples pray: Spirit of Jesus, come.

Verses 5-8 HARMONY

5. Sud-dedn-ly, de-scend-ing, rush of wind and flame; all in-spired, dis-ci-ples say:
6. Sud-den-ly, the church breaks forth in ev-'ry tongue; now with *hwyl* a-post-les say:
7. Now is sav-ing grace to young and old pro-claimed; end-less-ly, God's peo-ple say:
8. Sum-moned to be one, and gath-ered in your Name, joy-ful-ly to-day, we pray:

1. verses 5,6,7
Spir-it of Christ, wel - come!
Spir-it of Christ, well come!
Spir-it of Christ, is come.

last verse
Spir-it of Christ, lead on!

Descant verse 8
8. Sum-moned to be one, and gath-ered in your name, joy-ful-ly we pray: "Spir-it of Christ, lead on!"

78

C.W. Everest 1814-77

Doug Constable
© 1973/2012

EVEREST LM

(Musical score)

1. Take up thy cross, the Saviour said, if thou wouldst my disciple be; deny thyself, the world forsake, and humbly follow after me.

2. Take up thy cross: let not its weight fill thy weak spirit with alarm; his strength shall bear thy spirit up, and brace thy heart, and nerve thine arm.

3. Take up thy cross, nor heed the shame, nor let thy foolish pride rebel: the Lord for thee the cross endured, to save thy soul from death and hell.

4. Take up thy cross then in his strength, and calmly ev'ry danger brave; 'twill guide thee to a better home, and lead to vict'ry o'er the grave.

5. Take up thy cross, and follow Christ, nor think till death to lay it down; for only they who bear the cross may hope to wear the glorious crown.

6. To thee, great Lord, the One in Three, all praise for evermore ascend: O grant us in our home to see the heav'nly life that knows no end.

Mark 8.34-38

I was singing this hymn in my head to its most well-known setting BRESLAU. At the end a male voice chorus continued singing in my head, but now to a new tune ...

79

George Herbert
1593-1633

Doug Constable
© 1973

♩ = 88 As softly and gently as possible

Teach me, my God and King, in all things Thee to see; and what I do in any-thing, to do it as for Thee.

    Teach me, my God and King,
    in all things thee to see;
    and what I do in anything
    to do it as for thee.

    A man that looks on glass,
    on it may stay his eye;
    or, if he pleaseth, through it pass,
    and then the heaven espy.

    All may of thee partake;
    nothing can be so mean
    which, with this tincture, *For thy sake*,
    will not grow bright and clean.

    A servant with this clause
    makes drudgery divine;
    who sweeps a room, as for thy laws,
    makes that and the action fine.

    This is the famous stone
    that turneth all to gold;
    for that which God doth touch and own
    cannot for less be told.

2 Corinthians 5.19
This setting of Herbert's beloved words was composed for a dramatic presentation about St Paul, a meditation on his assertion, 'From now on, therefore, we regard no one from a human point of view…' The hushed, almost breathless, music makes space for feelings of deep reverence in the face of all that God gives and redeems.

Socially-distanced Christmas

Socially-distanced tenderness:
to human flesh the Word says Yes;
bubbles rejoice, and heaven comes close.

To masked-up souls God shows a face,
our breath she breathes, fills every place;
lockdowns and tiers host angels' peace.

Love, the antidote to fear,
vaccinates with holy cheer,
brings the season of safety near:
Jesus is born, the day is here!

Dear Christ, masses of hungry feast,
last to the fore, most serve the least:
Carers adore, all folks find rest:

Hearts to the stable! Prove Love's guest!

Christmas 2020

80

The Most High made a garden and made it out of love:
a holy arboretum, its roots in heaven above;
the tree of life God planted there – a cure for every woe –
    bound all around with angels' care,
    that all might thrive and grow,
    that all might thrive and grow.

Another tree in Eden put forth its fruit to view;
temptation called, 'Come, taste it, as gods be born anew';
and, eager for preferment - sweet life for evermore -
    we took the fruit, profaned its root,
    pushed selfhood to the fore,
    pushed selfhood to the fore.

But God in mercy sees us, all sunk in shame and fear,
and in our flesh restores us with love's deep lancing spear;
from out the bleeding heart of Christ, death's antidote is borne,
    and angels wait at heaven's gate
    each prodigal's return,
    each prodigal's return.

Now in love's Easter arbour fresh joys are daily grown:
all creatures reap rich harvest where once was sorrow known;
the commonwealth of care is lived, and all have their fair share,
    while Love endows, espouses, sows
    new gardens everywhere,
    new gardens everywhere.

Genesis 2.8-3.24; Romans 5.6-10; John 19.33-37
The original of this was written for the Mothers' Union of St Thomas' Peartree, Derby, to sing on Mothering Sunday 1979; but I failed to keep a copy. The first four lines are as the original; the rest of the text is a new composition. The tune is as first composed, though with harmony now added. The Arboretum in the next-door parish of St James' is the oldest municipally-funded park in England.

ARBORETUM 13 13 14 8 6 6

Words and Music
Doug Constable
© 1979/2012

♩ = 104

The Most High made a garden and formed it out of love: a holy arboretum, its roots in heaven above; the tree of life God planted there, a cure for ev'ry woe, bound all around with angel's care, that all might thrive and grow, that all might thrive and grow.

2. Another tree in Eden put forth its fruit to view; temptation called, 'Come, taste it, as gods be born anew.' And, eager for preferment sweet life for evermore, we took the fruit, profaned its root, pushed selfhood to the fore, pushed selfhood to the fore.

3. But God in mercy sees us, all sunk in shame and fear; and in our flesh restores us with love's deep lancing spear; from out the bleeding heart of Christ death's antidote is borne, and angels wait at heaven's gate each prodigal's return, each prodigal's return.

4. Now in love's Easter arbour fresh joys are daily grown: all creatures reap rich harvest where once was sorrow known; the commonwealth of care is lived, and all have their fair share, while Love endows, espouses, sows new gardens ev'rywhere, new garden ev'rywhere.

81

Words and Music
Doug Constable
© 1996

TITUS 6666
♩ = 92

1. The source of life at first all being seethed and spawned: now in this world at last the grace of God has dawned.
2. We see by heaven's light this friends but grace made blood and bone and stabled in our heart till all our striving's done.
3. What shall we do, then, but praise this life of grace till all the world re-sounds with people making peace?

The source of life at first
   all being seethed and spawned:
now in this world at last
   the grace of God has dawned.

We see by heaven's light
   this grace made blood and bone
and stabled in our heart
   till all our healing's done.

What shall we do then, friends,
   but praise this life of grace
till all the world resounds
   with people making peace?

Titus 2.11
The words of this hymn, written to be sung on Christmas Day, respond to the proclamation that the grace of God has dawned upon the world with healing for all humankind.
The harmonic shifts in the fourth line of music (the melody is on just one note) hint at the humanly inconceivable change that has come upon the cosmos with the birth of Christ.

ST DWYNWEN'S DAY

When Maelon's marrying suit was turned to ice,
and Dwynwen prayed for him, then took the veil,
it seemed perverse, the shaking of life's dice
that made her patron saint of love in Wales.
For all the world, 'tis said, loves lovers, hates
to see them baulked, frustrated their desires;
the Welsh, it seems, can smile at frowning fates,
cheer up sad maids and comfort pining squires.
Since God un-froze the berg of Maelon's pain,
blesses the hopes and dreams of lovers true,
and since, as Dwynwen prays, spring stirs again –
shows snowdrops, singing birds, in couples too –
this maladroit old rhymester, cap in hand,
knocks at your door, and waits on love's command.

25.1.2019

BILLET DOUX

Dear blessed Sister Dwynwen, bride of Christ,
I hope this finds you well, heart on the wing.
Your Maelon greets you kindly, not surprised
you took the veil, rather than wear my ring.
At first I was aggrieved, I must confess,
for I desired your will, your self, your all;
I did not understand, nor could I guess
you'd flower best enclosed behind a wall.
But I have lately come to see that 'wife'
means thriving safe and free in boundless space,
that there's a heavenly Spouse claims each one's life –
mine too – for cherishing in warm embrace.
I know I've been an ice-man far too long;
the weather's turned now. So has my love-song.

23.1.2021

82

There is a gift we cannot grasp
but humbly may receive:
the grace that only love can clasp
and share, truth to achieve.

This gift is called the Eden tree,
that good and evil knows;
who tend it root and branch set free
the grace that in them grows.

Yet none has waited till the fruit
should find in each its home,
but all have wrenched it from its root
to make their pleasure come.

Thus, good is ours, but evil too,
while Eden stands alone;
defiant, and ashamed, we rue
the deed, the grief we've sown.

By Eden's tree there stands a cross
where love was crucified
to save us from eternal loss,
to raise us up who've died.

Therefore into the wilderness
we go, to face the worst;
we learn to wait in love, to bless
the love for whom we thirst.

Genesis 2.15-17; 3.1-7 and Matthew 4.1-11.
Here is a meditation on the so-called 'fall of humankind'. God invites us freely to eat *of every tree of the garden* except *the tree of the knowledge of good and evil*, whose fruit is given by grace alone.
Composed on the day when Christina Rossetti is celebrated, the music is in the style of a gentle folk-song (echoing the opening of the Somerset song 'Waly Waly').

Words and Music
Doug Constable
© 2001

CHRISROSS CM

♩ = 80 Flowing

1. There is a gift we can-not grasp but hum-bly may re-ceive:
   called the Ed-en tree, that good and ev-il knows;
   wait-ed till the fruit should find in each its home,

the grace that on-ly love can clasp and share, truth
who tend it root and branch set free the grace that
but all have wrenched it from its root to make their

1.2.3
to ach-ieve.
in them grows.
pleas-ure come.

2. This gift is
3. Yet none has

4.
acc.

194

4. Thus, good is ours, but evil too, while Eden stands alone; defiant, and ashamed, we rue the deed, the grief we've sown.

5. By Eden's tree there stands a cross where love was crucified to save us from eternal loss, to raise us up who've died.

6. Therefore in to the wilderness we go, to face the worst; we learn to wait in love, and bless the love for whom we thirst.

SUNDAY MORNING A WHILE AGO

I heard a Presbyterian preacher say,
"Before the service, speak to God.
In the service, let God speak to you.
Speak to each other afterward."

We'd not been there before. We had to park
some distance away. Arrived five minutes early.
Inside, were greeted with a silent smile
and given books. We turned into the tiny
nave, and instantly were overcome
by quiet, people praying, people waiting
patiently for God to come. Hardly
we dared find a place, lest we disturb.

During the service, comfort gradually
enfolded us within the company.
By the end, the 'Go in peace to love
and serve the Lord', we felt at ease, met others
gladly. Driving home, we knew we'd been
guests at the Lamb's high feast, served in that church.

2014

83

There is a love more perfect than all the loves of earth,
that, springing like a fountain, brings everything to birth.
It lives in every creature, in all the human race;
it suffers every mortal grief, and feels the world's disgrace.
Oppressed, yet never conquered, forever strong and free,
this love is Christ incarnate transfiguring you and me.

With love we shape our journey, we live with loss and gain;
we strive to hold together our years of joy and pain.
But we are also broken – we spoil the earth's rich store;
we therefore seek forgiveness, and ask that love restore
each sister and each brother to grow in Christ our peace,
that all may thrive in fullness, and common wealth increase.

To Love most high, most glorious, eternal, faithful, true;
to Love enfleshed, embodied – a story always new;
to Love that kindles in us the fires of faith each day:
to Three-in-One united with humble thanks we pray
that every living creature, both now, and yet to be,
may serve on earth God's purpose, and share Love's victory.

At St Martin's Junior School in Dorking we used to sing *I vow to thee my country* (by Cecil Spring-Rice 1859-1918 to music specially written for it – ABINGER - by local resident Ralph Vaughan Williams 1872-1958; and I loved that song, both the music and the words. Only when I got into the wider world did I discover that no-one sings *I vow to thee* to the tune ABINGER; THAXTED being preferred by RVW's friend, Gustav Holst 1874-1934.
I was a chorister at St Martin's Church, Dorking, and, when the Hymn Society planned to hold a festival there, I wrote these words to be sung to ABINGER, hoping that tune might thereby become better known and loved.

Doug Constable 2006

R. Vaughan Williams
1872-1958

ABINGER

1. There is a love more perfect than all the loves of earth, that, springing from a fountain, brings ev'rything to birth. It lives in ev'ry creature, in all the human race; it
2. With love we shape our journey, we live with loss and gain; we strive to hold together our years of joy and pain. But we are also broken: we spoil the earth's rich store; we
3. To Love most high, most glorious, eternal, faithful, true; to Love enfleshed, embodied: a story always new; to Love that kindles in us the fires of faith each day: to

Words copyright 2006

suf - fers ev - 'ry mortal grief. and feels the world's dis - grace. Op - pressed, yet nev - er
there - fore seek for - give - ness, and ask that love re - store each sis - ter and each
Three - in - One u - nit - ed with humble thanks we pray that ev - 'ry liv - ing

con quered, for ev - er strong and free, this love is Christ in - car - nate trans
broth - er to grow in Christ our peace, that all may thrive in full - ness. and
creat - ure, both now and yet to be, may serve on earth God's pur - pose, and

fig - 'ring you and me.
com - mon - wealth in - crease.
share Love's vic - tor - y.

84

Words and Music
Doug Constable
© 2003

KIPPETT CM ♩ = 96

1. There's laughter in the loins of those who make love's home on earth; God's Spirit seeds the womb with praise, and smiles of joy spring forth.
2. No wanton thought, God's laughing heart, no random whim or jest: love's purpose is creation's fate, and heav'n wills earth to feast.
3. The source of laughter's child implants its seeds where wells have dried; and many ageing, weary saints grow young where grace has played.
4. But many more, deprived, disgraced, have never known your smile; let them by mercy thrive, enticed to praise you in life's soil.
5. Dear Father, Holy Mother, One In-spiriting all lives: come visit, bless, each woman, man with laughing love that saves.

200

There's laughter in the loins of those
who make love's home on earth;
God's spirit seeds the womb with praise,
and smiles of joy spring forth.

No wanton thought, God's laughing heart,
no random whim or jest:
love's purpose is creation's fate;
heaven wills all earth to feast.

The source of laughter's child implants
its seed where wells have dried;
and many ageing weary saints
grow young where grace has played.

But many more, deprived, disgraced,
have never known your smile;
let them by mercy thrive, enticed
to praise you in life's soil.

Dear Father, Holy Mother, One
Inspiriting all lives:
come visit, bless each woman, man
with laughing love that saves.

Genesis 18.1-15
We are told that the name Isaac means 'God has smiled' or 'God laughs'. Understandably, ninety-year old Sarai laughed when she overheard God's messengers telling her one hundred-year old husband that she, Sarai, was to give birth to a son.
Seeing how to write a hymn from this story about a couple well into retirement was difficult until I recalled Keith TIPPETT reminding me that the way to make God laugh is by announcing your plans for the future…
Although it can certainly be for ageing lovers, this hymn is offered to all who "make love's home on earth".

85

Lewis Hensley 1824-1905
HENSLEY 6666

Doug Constable
© 1973

Thy kingdom come, O God,
thy rule, O Christ begin;
break with thine iron rod
the tyrannies of sin.

Where is thy reign of peace
and purity and love?
When shall all hatred cease,
as in the realms above?

When comes the promised time
that war shall be no more,
and lust, oppression, crime
shall flee thy face before?

We pray thee, Lord, arise,
and come in thy great might;
revive our longing eyes,
which languish for thy sight.

Men scorn thy sacred Name,
and wolves devour thy fold;
by many deeds of shame
we learn that love grows cold.

O'er lands both near and far
thick darkness broodeth yet:
arise, O Morning Star,
arise, and never set.

This setting was made to serve as prelude to a music drama about the ministry, death, and resurrection of Christ. It is intentionally set rather high in in unison voices, to suggest an almost febrile desperation in the world's ongoing prayer to be saved from 'lust, oppression, crime'.

86

This body, Lord, is mine and yours;
this life, your settled home, is mine.
In you I travel all my course;
your presence makes my self divine.

This muscle, Lord, this dated bone,
these limbs, these organs, and this face,
all wonderfully together grown,
present as this, your body's grace.

Lord Jesus Christ, in you this cell,
this pulse, this love en-fleshed, is more:
incorporate we are. We dwell
all present, in each other's core.

Be present, Lord, in this our time,
in this, our body's sacrifice;
may we in all things wholly rhyme
with mercy's God, pay love's full price.

Romans 12.1; 1 Corinthians 12.27
Throughout history many Christians have viewed the body with suspicion, choosing to value the spirit above the body. This hymn consciously queers such a view, affirming instead what the novelist Paul Scott called 'the body's grace'. The 3rd verse is a brief meditation on the affirmation that we are *the body of Christ, and individually members of it*. Dwelling "all present, in each other's core" subversively suggests a more radical belonging to each other than is typically assumed.
The music is also slightly subversive, a bit nervous, faintly voluptuous. It feels precarious, but is actually not out of control; for, despite sliding chromatic scales, the music never leaves its home key.

QUEER 8888

Words and Music
Doug Constable
© 2002

♩ = 104 Slow foxtrot

1. This body, Lord, is mine and yours; this life, your settled home, is mine. In you I travel all my course; your presence makes myself divine.

2. This muscle, Lord, this dated bone, these limbs, these organs, and this face, all wonder'f'ly together grown, present as this, your body's grace.

3. Lord Jesus Christ, in you this cell, this pulse, this love enfleshed is more:

204

The Deanery House Southampton
for Gillian Limb, and for Sue Orton

[Set to the theme of the Adagietto from Mahler's 5th Symphony]

Within this city
there blooms a flower
that's rooted deep in Eden's garden,
where peace and pardon
are served as word and sacrament of love.

Within this flower
caring and pity
for those who call,
with hospitality for all.
It is the prayer of love.

Out of Eden
there flows a river
through the city:
none can stay
its living way;
and day by day,
through all who pray
and bless, caress, the city,
life
is borne anew,
and comes to rest.

Thanks for the city,
and for the river,
and for the flower that blooms in heaven.

September 1996

87

This night the grace of God has conquered!
let all creation raise the shout!
the love that made us all has triumphed,
and Christ turns hell all inside out!
From lasting death to joy for ever,
our Light now rises high,
and shines through lives brought over
who praise this glorious victory.

Our hearts refuse all paths of evil,
that every soul may thrive aright
and see God's Loved One, rising, revel
in rays of resurrection light.
As waters break, new creatures birthing,
and hope soars strong and free,
see where high heaven comes earthing,
while sovereign love reigns on life's tree.

So let the universe be joyful!
resounding earth her song begin!
from sin redeemed, sinners united –
the Church, and all that is therein!
All instruments, all bodies, voices
in nature's anthems blend;
and all the world rejoices,
for saving love now has no end.

1 Corinthians 15.20b, 22 John 12.32
The music was composed at Lee Abbey to set 'The day of resurrection' by St John of Damascus (c675-c750) at the end of a dramatic presentation of Jesus' Passion. At the first performance the melody was played over in the dark by a solo trumpeter, whose home was in RAYLEIGH, Essex. The music was written so that a stately procession could be danced to it, depicting the universe exulting at Easter.
Written for the ceremonies of the Easter Vigil, the new-minted words of the later lyric are closely based on those of St John's hymn. In verse 2 "God's Loved One" is an attempt to encapsulate all that is signified by the Scriptural phrases Son of Man and Son of God.
"As waters break…" uses imagery of birth to draw attention to the renewal of baptismal vows that takes place at this service.

RAYLEIGH 9898 9678

♩ = 104 Very broad. Whole line phrase

Words 2001
Music 1974
Doug Constable ©

1. This night the grace of God has conquered! Let all creation raise the shout! The love that made us all has triumphed, and Christ turns hell all inside out! From lasting death to joy for ever, our

ev'ry soul may thrive aright, and see God's Loved One, rising, revel in rays of resurrection light. As waters break, new creatures birthing, and

sounding earth her song begin! from sin redeemed, sinners united: the Church, and all that sin is therein! All instruments, all bodies, voices in

Light now rises high, and shines through lives brought over to praise this glorious victory.
hope soars strong and free, where high heav'n comes earthing, sov-reign love reigns from life's tree.
nat-re's anthems blend, and see all the world rejoices, while for saving love now has no end

2. Our hearts refuse all paths of evil, that
3. So let the universe be joyful, re

88

B.S. Ingermann (1789-1862) trans. S. Baring-Gould
ROBINLEE 8787

Doug Constable
© 1974

♩ = 132 Trudging, but not dragging

Through the night of doubt and sor-row
UNISON
on-ward goes the pil-grim band,
sing-ing songs of ex-al-ta-tion,
HARMONY
march-ing to the pro-mised land, the pro-mised land.
   -ing to the pro-mised land, the pro-mised land.

Last verse
rit
gloom, the end of toil and gloom, the end of toil and gloom.
gloom, the end of gloom.

Through the night of doubt and sorrow
onward goes the pilgrim band,
singing songs of exaltation,
marching to the promised land.

Clear before us through the darkness
gleams and burns the guiding light:
each one clasps the hand of other,
stepping fearless through the night.

One the light of God's own presence
o'er his ransomed people shed,
chasing far the gloom and terror,
brightening all the path we tread.

One the object of our journey,
one the faith which never tires,
one the earnest looking forward,
one the hope our God inspires.

One the strain which lips of thousands
lift as from the heart of one;
one the conflict, one the peril,
one the march in God begun.

One the gladness of rejoicing
on the far eternal shore,
where the one almighty Father
reigns in love for evermore.

Onward, pilgrims, sisters, brothers,
onward with the cross our aid;
bear its shame, and fight its battle,
till we rest beneath its shade.

Soon shall come the great awaking,
soon the rending of the tomb;
and the scattering of all shadows,
and the end of toil and gloom.

An as-it-were chorale for travellers to Bethlehem in the Nativity-tableau *Wrestling with Christ*. The emphasis in this music is on both the long trudge through doubt and sorrow, and the guiding light gleaming through the darkness.

89

AGNES 7676
♩ = 92

Words and Music
Doug Constable
© 1997

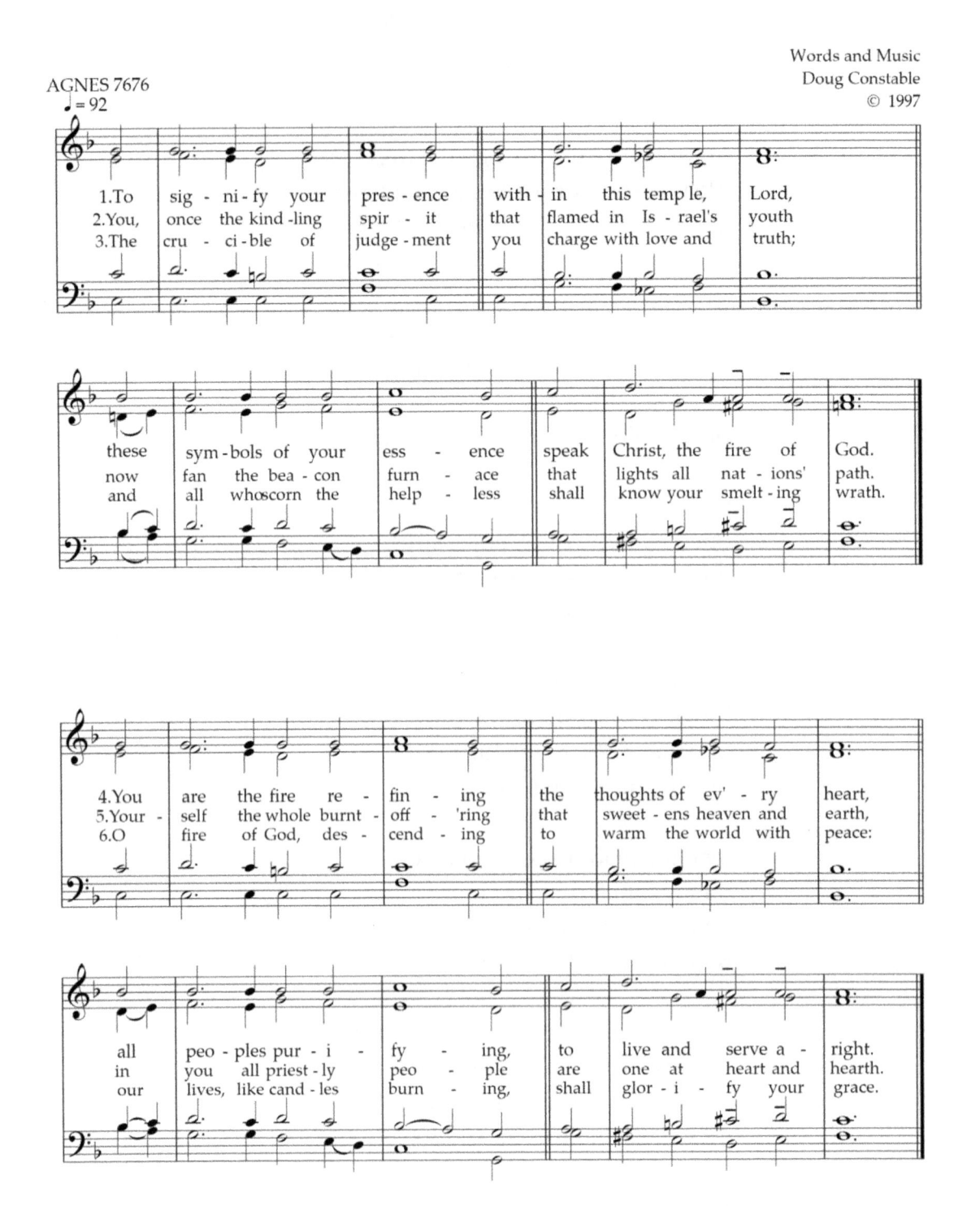

1. To signify your presence within this temple, Lord,
these symbols of your essence speak Christ, the fire of God.

2. You, once the kindling spirit that flamed in Israel's youth
now fan the beacon furnace that lights all nations' path.

3. The crucible of judgement you charge with love and truth;
and all who scorn the helpless shall know your smelting wrath.

4. You are the fire refining the thoughts of ev'ry heart,
all peoples purifying, to live and serve aright.

5. Yourself the whole burnt-off'ring that sweetens heaven and earth,
in you all priestly people are one at heart and hearth.

6. O fire of God, descending to warm the world with peace:
our lives, like candles burning, shall glorify your grace.

To signify your presence
within this temple Lord
these symbols of your essence
speak Christ, the fire of God.

You, once the kindling spirit
that flamed in Israel's youth,
now fan the beacon furnace
that lights all nations' path

The crucible of judgement
you charge with love and truth
and all who scorn the helpless
shall know your smelting wrath

You are the fire refining
the thoughts of every heart,
all peoples purifying,
to live and serve aright.

Yourself the whole burnt-offering
that sweetens heaven and earth,
in you all priestly people
are one at heart and hearth.

O fire of God, descending
to warm the world with peace:
our lives, like candles burning,
shall glorify your grace.

Luke 2.22-40
This hymn celebrates the Feast of the Presentation of Christ in the Temple, popularly known as Candlemas. Begun on St AGNES' Day, the music proceeds in stately fashion for two lines, moving towards an abrupt change of style in the fourth line: a conscious attempt to evoke the fiery otherness of Christ.

90

Charles Wesley 1707-1788

Doug Constable
© 1973

REAL PRESENCE 88 88 88

♩ = 108 Broad and flowing

1. Victim Divine, Thy grace we claim, While thus Thy precious death we show: Once offer'd up, a spotless Lamb, In Thy great temple here below, Thou didst for all mankind atone, And standest now before the Throne.

2. Thou standest in the holiest place, As now for guilty sinners slain; Thy blood of sprinkling speaks and prays All-prevalent for helpless man; Thy blood is still our ransom found, And spreads salvation all around.

3. We need not now go up to Heav'n To bring the long-sought Saviour down; Thou art to all that seek Thee giv'n, Thou dost e'en now Thy banquet crown; To ev'ry faithful soul appear, And show Thy Real Presence here.

Charles Wesley's words were set for a dramatic presentation at Lee Abbey about the Holy Eucharist. Inspired by Jan (c1395-c1441) and Hubert (d.1426) Van Eyck's painting *The Adoration of the Holy Lamb* (in the cathedral at Ganf/Ghent), few congregations will want to attempt this lofty setting! The musical style is intended to evoke both 'things of heaven and earth in our midst' and the immensity of what is accomplished in Christ's Atoning Sacrifice.

THE LONG WATCH ON HOLOCAUST MEMORIAL DAY

Upon the cross love's heroes hang,
hate's victims every day;
their suffering is redemption's song,
their offering, life's hard way.

Slain by an evil stalking all,
they live before God's face
(for there's no soul can ever fall
beyond high heaven's embrace).

Some give themselves into God's hands,
while others die in rage;
some die like sacrificial lambs,
and some breathe sacrilege.

But each asks we be there with them,
to own the cross each day,
in Christ to bear the sin and shame,
in peace to learn to pray.

Do stay, love asks us, by the cross,
and count it joy to grieve,
for there compassion finds increase,
shows how we may forgive.

The fiery cross turns all to ash;
all memories will wane;
but love speaks from the burning bush:
keep faith, and live again.

The commonwealth of peace on earth
waits on our humble Yes:
so choose the cross, embrace new birth,
bless God; and pray, God bless.

27.1.2018

91

Words and Music:
Doug Constable
1986

GRIMES 8 10 8 9

♩ = 56

1. Warm God of seeds, all nature's source, Womb of earth-maker, and love's stirring pulse, sown in our soil, your-self conceived: grant we may rev'rence each life you give.

2. Dark God of roots, of nurture, growth, ancestors' bedrock, and wisdom's new path, breaking all ground, your-self the light: grant we respect all who seek for light.

3. Shared God of hearts, forth-branching stem, all creatures' measure, and history's frame: stretched on our wood, you died in pain; grant we restore all who sink in shame.

4. Full God of blood, to oceans sprung, passion's fruit-blossom, and Christ-sounding song, fused through our veins, your-self heav'n's price: grant ev'ry creature your peace embrace.

© Stainer & Bell 1993 HARMONY © Doug Constable 2021

Warm God of seeds, all nature's source,
womb-of-earth maker, and love's stirring pulse,
sown in our soil, your self conceived:
grant we may reverence each life you give.

Dark God of roots, of nurture, growth,
ancestors' bedrock, and wisdom's path,
breaking all ground, yourself the light:
grant we respect all who seek for sight.

Shared God of hearts, forth-branching stem,
all creatures' measure, and history's frame:
stretched on our wood, you died in pain;
grant we restore all who sink in shame.

Full God of blood, to oceans sprung,
passion's fruit-blossom, and Christ-surged song,
fused through our veins, yourself heaven's price:
grant every creature your peace embrace.

© Copyright 1993 Stainer & Bell Ltd, 23 Gruneisen Road, London N3 1LS, www.stainer.co.uk. Used by permission. All rights reserved.

Colossians 1.15-20
 I was one of the helpers at an Interfaith Celebration in Assisi to mark the 25th anniversary of what was then called the World Wildlife Fund. This hymn was written for a report of the event to a meeting in Southampton. It also can be found in *Reflecting Praise* (© Stainer & Bell and Women in Theology 1993).
The start of the music copies a principal motif from the third of the Four Sea Interludes in Benjamin Britten's *Peter GRIMES*.

FORZADEST 88 88

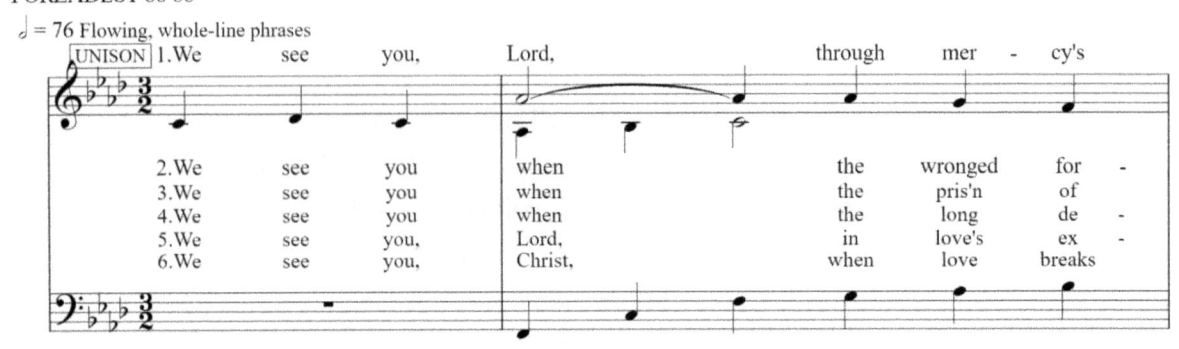

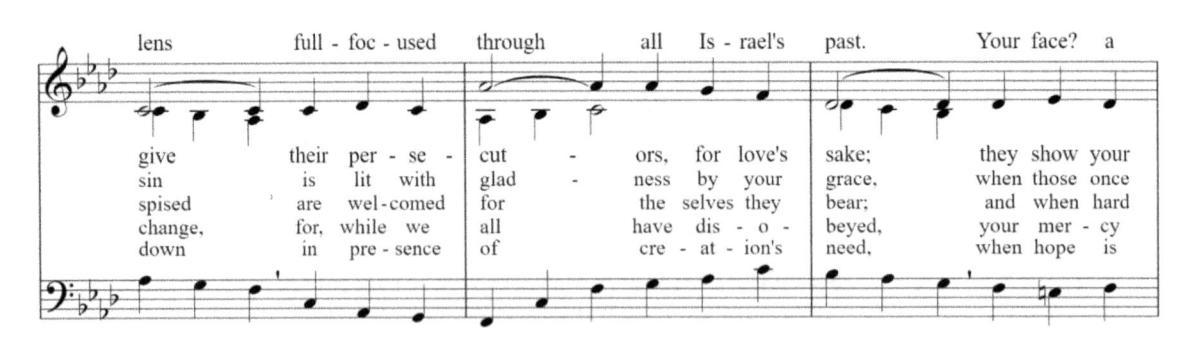

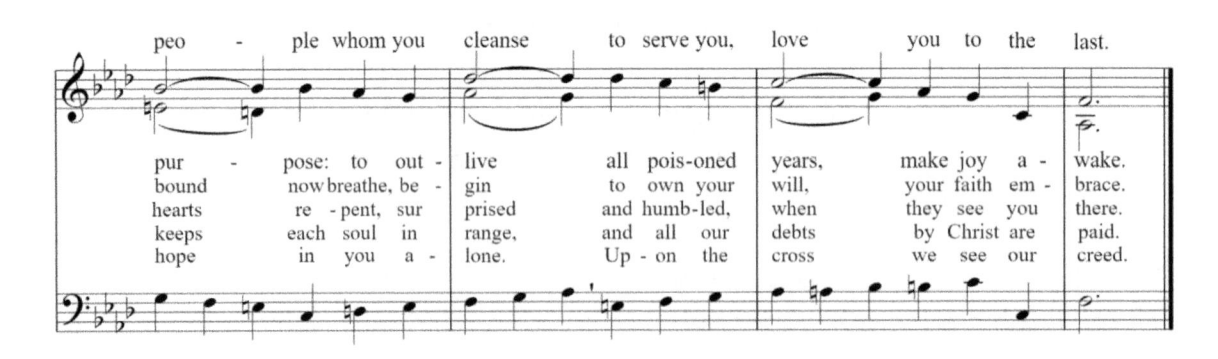

Words and Music
Doug Constable
© 2002

♩ = 76 Flowing, whole-line phrases

1. We see you, Lord, through mercy's lens full-focused through all Israel's past. Your face? a people whom you cleanse to serve you, love you to the last.

2. We see you when the wronged forgive their persecutors, for love's sake; they show your purpose: to outlive all poisoned years, make joy awake.

3. We see you when the pris'n of sin is lit with gladness by your grace, when those once bound now breathe, begin to own your will, your faith embrace.

4. We see you when the long despised are welcomed for the selves they bear; and when hard hearts repent, surprised and humbled, when they see you there.

5. We see you, Lord, in love's expanse, while we all have disobeyed, your mercy keeps each soul in range, and all our debts by Christ are paid.

6. We see you, Christ, when love breaks down in presence of creation's need, when hope is gone, in you alone. Upon the cross we see our creed.

We see you, Lord, through mercy's lens
full-focused through all Israel's past.
Your face? a people whom you cleanse
to serve you, love you to the last.

We see you when the wronged forgive
their persecutors for love's sake;
they show your purpose: to outlive
all poisoned years, make joy awake.

We see you when the prison of sin
is lit with gladness by your grace,
when those once bound now breathe, begin
to own your will, your faith embrace.

We see you when the long despised
are welcomed for the selves they bear,
and when hard hearts repent, surprised
and humbled, when they see you there.

We see you, Lord, in love's exchange,
for, while we all have disobeyed,
your mercy keeps each soul in range,
and all our debts by Christ are paid.

We see you, Christ, when love breaks down
in presence of creation's need,
when hope is hope in you alone.
Upon the cross we see our creed.

Genesis 45.1-15; Romans 11.1-2a, 29-32; Matthew 15.21-28
The theme of this hymn is God's sovereign mercy. Its contents come from three sources: Verse 1 alludes to Paul's discussion of Israel's place in God's providence; Verses 2-3 derive from the story of the reconciliation between Joseph and his brothers; Verse 4 is from the story of the healing of a Canaanite woman's daughter. The first two lines of the melody quote from Act 4 of Verdi's opera 'La FORZA della Destino'. A doleful fate for the world can be softened and, we believe, undone by the mercy that flows from the cross of God in Christ.

93

When in the wastes of wild regret,
when shame shuts down your mind,
when caught in memory's closing net,
and all your life seems blind:
lift up the serpent of your sin,
lift up the fate you fear,
and look upon the way wherein
th'eternal age draws near.

For now's the time when one good soul,
God's own, of woman born,
is lifted on the serpent's pole,
and bears our pain and scorn.
The time has come that faith foretold,
that hope reached out for long,
when love is given as new for old,
and Christ undoes all wrong.

Let all the world look on the face
that wears all history's woes;
let all the world find there the grace
whence life's full healing flows.
For every well of rage and grief
that floods into love's sea
returns in power as joy's belief:
in Christ God sets us free.

Words: Doug Constable © 2004
Music: KINGSFOLD
from *English Country Songs 1893*
Metre: DCM

Numbers 21.4-9; John 12.32-33
This was written as part of a Lenten sermon for the congregation of St Anne's Calmore near Southampton.

94

What kind of human commands the sea,
  compels the winds to obey?
What kind of being can save you and me,
  and every power amaze?
What kind of master can sleep through a storm,
  his vessel set to capsize?
What kind of sovereign redeems from all harm
  all souls, to be love's prize?

Let every creature resound God's praise,
  who rules both winds and sea!
Let every people the Name upraise
  of a Saviour who sets us free!
Let the redeemed from all fear declare
  Christ's peace all around, within!
Let the new-abled in every place
  new life in Christ begin!

Mark 4.35-40
When Bishop John PERRY instituted Eileen Wetherell to be Vicar of CALMORE he preached about Jesus calming the storm on the lake. This piece commemorates the occasion.

CALPERRYMORE 9 6 10 7 10 7 10 7

Words and Music
Doug Constable
© 1996

♩ = 100

What kind of hu-man com mands the sea, com-pels the waves to o- bey?

What kind of be-ing can save you and me, and ev'-ry power a- maze?

What kind of mast-er can sleep through a storm, his ves-sel set to cap size?

What kind of sovreign re deems from all harm all souls, to be love's prize?

Let ev'ry creature resound God's praise, who rules both winds and sea!

Let ev'ry people the Name up-raise of a Saviour who sets us free!

Let the redeemed from all fear declare Christ's peace all around, within!

Let the new-abled in ev'ry place new life in Christ begin!

95

PENICILLIN 4 LM

Words and Music:
Doug Constable
© 2001/14

♩ = 92

1. When terror strikes, when gun or bomb contests each claim to peace on earth: be with the maimed, th'aggrieved, the numb; declare each creature's priceless worth.

2. When terror strikes, when right or wrong presumes to force its way to power, be with the weak, as with the strong; inspire new hope, new love to flower.

3. When terror strikes, when greed or lust pretends to wear the face of life, be with the robbed, the raped, the lost, restore their pride, from give rest strife.

4. When terror strikes, let worth, love, pride absorb the worst that death can bring, let justice roll, and mercy ride on waves of truth, till all may sing:

When terror strikes, when gun or bomb
contests each claim to peace on earth,
be with the maimed, th'aggrieved, the numb;
declare each creature's priceless worth.

When terror strikes, when right or wrong
presumes to force its will to power,
be with the weak, as with the strong;
inspire new hope, new love to flower.

When terror strikes, when greed or lust
pretends to wear the face of life,
be with the robbed, the raped, the lost,
restore their pride, and end their strife.

When terror strikes, let worth, love, pride
absorb the worst that death can bring;
let justice roll, and mercy ride
on waves on truth, till all may sing:

Now terror's done: the heart's new day
enables all to start again
and flourish as all humans may –
each girl and boy, each woman, man.

Now glory's won: all cosmic chance
subsists within love's wounded frame.
We bear our truth, our faith we dance:
The Crucified and Risen we name.

Jim Cotter (1942-2014) offered alternatives to the last two stanzas

Pierce every heart with penitence
for violence done, or good withheld;
remove the masks of cold pretence,
and vengeance once for all repel.

The vision holds: pain, evil, death
by wounded love are swallowed up.
New life takes wing on every breath;
old foes now share a common cup.

Psalm 79.1-4 Luke 23.43
This was composed three weeks after the destruction of the World Trade Centre in New York. I consciously tried to work the sound of emergency services sirens into the music. It is not easy to know how to go on from the trauma of terror, as my last two verses illustrate.

UPSTAIRS-DOWNSTAIRS
for Angela

I had a word with Him Upstairs:
my word was *Please,* the word I spoke and prayed.

No answer came at first;
I heard no answer for a long, long time,
while, echoing, my word trundled
up and down the tunnel of my days and nights.

At length –
and in the depth of my heart's winter -
snowdrops began to smile again,
my eyes not taking No for an answer.
My taste-buds opened one by one,
traces of fragrances nosily eased their ways;
a finger-touching set my pimples all-a-goose together.

That was when
I heard my word
come back to me,
not from cold stone,
not like a letter unopened,
but wrapped in tender overtones
from Yourself Upstairs:
a word as sure as eggs are broken,
as sure as dumptied love is once more put together.

My word and yours I put together then –
my *Please,* your *Sure* –
mine going up, yours coming down a rainbow.
The sound, it gave me *pleasure,* which, within my ears
was most assuring, as though
our words would always from now on
go back and forth between us,
heart speaking to heart.

You came down
to give me Your word,
and so we bandied words together …

2010

96

'Where is he?' the wise men asking,
'We have travelled far to find,
Leaving ease and great position
At the bidding of the mind.'
No-one in the city knew him,
At the inn the lip was curled;
In a shakedown in the garage
Lay the Saviour of the world.

Halted we, and knelt in glory
At the royal infant's cry.
Morning brought the clang of dustbins,
City cleaners passing by.
Long we knelt in adoration,
In the inn the dancers swirled;
In a shakedown in the garage
Lay the Saviour of the world.

Gently in her arms she bore him,
Virgin-Mother's only child;
Born that we might be redeemed,
God and man be reconciled.
Brothers, sisters, join to greet him,
To the skies your praises hurled;
In a shakedown in the garage
Lay the Saviour of the world.

Words: James Fraser

Words © 1968 Stainer & Bell Ltd, 23 Gruneisen Road, London N3 1LS, UK, www.stainer.co.uk. Used by permission.

Matthew 2.1-2
When I first read these words I had just heard George Harrison's "Within you Without you" on the newly released *Sergeant Pepper's Lonely Hearts Club Band* album. My setting was written as a conscious parody of Harrison's piece, and it was with some embarrassment that I subsequently offered it as an ensemble hymn. But at Lee Abbey a chorus of young adults sang it vigorously and with evident joy.
In the fifth line of the third stanza I have altered the original to make the lyric inclusive.

James Fraser
© 1968 Stainer & Bell

Doug Constable
© 1969

WITHOUTGEOHAR 87 87 87 86

1. 'Where is he?' the wise men asking, 'we have travelled far to find, leaving ease and great position at the bidding of the mind.' No-one in the ci-
2. Halted we, and knelt in glory at the royal infant's cry. Morning brought the clang of dust-bins, cleaners passing by. Long we knelt in a-
3. Gently in her arms she bore him, Virgin Mother's only child; Born that we might be redeemed, God and man be reconciled. Brothers, sisters, join

228

- ty knew him, At the inn the lip was curled; In a shake-down
- dor - a - tion, In the inn the dan-cers swirled In a shake-down
to greet him, To the skies your prais-es hurled: In a shake-down
in the gar - age lay the Sav - iour of the
in the gar - age lay the Sav - iour of the
in the gar - age lay the Sav - iour lay the
1.2.
world.
world.
3.
Sav - iour, lay the Sav - iour
of the world.
molto rit.

97

BOYCEHILL 55 44 85 4

Words and Music
Doug Constable
© 1996

1. Whoever you are, whatever your state, to you there comes this day, this night, from way beyond your dearest dreams good will from heaven, the best of times.

2. Whoever you are, wherever you be, the news is ripe for you to know: from one step to find new-born, at hand: a child of heaven, a saviour, friend.

3. Whoever you are, however you cope, it's not too far for you to stoop to love this child, the soul of peace, with all of heaven to praise this grace.

Whoever you are,
whatever your state,
to you there comes
this day, this night
from way beyond
your dearest dreams
goodwill from heaven,
the best of times.

Whoever you are,
wherever you be,
the news is ripe
for you to know:
one step to find
new-born, at hand,
a child of heaven,
a saviour, friend.

Whoever you are,
however you cope,
it's not too far
for you to stoop
to love this child,
the soul of peace,
with all of heaven
to praise this grace.

Luke 2.8-18
The Christmas angels proclaim their message to (literally) poor shepherds. In this hymn, as in much other reflection on that story, the shepherds represent all of humanity, individually and collectively.
The hymn was first sung at a conducting course led by June BOYCE-Tillman and David HILL.

98

Words and Music
Doug Constable
© 2002/21

Y BWTHYN 11 11 11 11

1. With fervent thanksgiving and joy in my heart, sure I am that nothing from God can us part, Whose love in Christ Jesus gives grace to unite: in Christ we are conqu'rors; in Christ we delight.

2. Yet grief is unceasing; there's pain in my heart; my dear ones are choosing to live set apart. To win back my people I'd forfeit my place, though God's blest Messiah has saved me by grace.

3. Here prayer means a struggle to hold in my heart God's love for all creatures whom fear drives apart. I will not desert them, though I be disgraced, for bonded together we all are embraced.

4. Dear God of all Israel (the joy of your heart), to whom You gave tokens that all have their part: encompass with blessing the last and the first: let all feast before you, your peace quench our thirst.

232

With fervent thanksgiving
and joy in my heart,
I am certain that nothing
from God can us part,
Whose love in Christ Jesus
gives grace to unite:
in Christ we are conquerors;
in Christ we delight.

Yet grief is unceasing;
there's pain in my heart:
my dear ones are choosing
to live set apart.
To win back my people,
I'd forfeit my place,
though God's blest Messiah
has saved me by grace.

Here prayer means a struggle
to hold in my heart
God's love for all creatures
whom fear drives apart:
I will not desert them,
though I be disgraced,
for, bonded together,
we all are embraced.

Dear God of all Israel
(the joy of your heart),
to whom you gave tokens
that all have their part:
encompass with blessing
the last and the first:
let all feast before you,
your peace quench our thirst.

Romans 8.39, 9.1-5, 11.1-2a
I have been trying to write this hymn for nearly twenty years, and I'm not sure if it's yet as it should be. In it singers take on the voice of Paul, a Jew first, then a Jewish Christian. At issue is how we understand *us* in Paul's testimony *I am convinced that … nothing in all creation will be able to separate us …* Those who read *us* as all-inclusive doubt that any creature or person is excluded from God's love.
This is the first music I wrote in the cottage Y BWTHYN that became our home in Wales.

99

Words and Music:
Doug Constable
© 1995 (after L. van Beethoven)

NINTH SEA BREEZE CM D

♩ = 104

1. Within the commonwealth of God all creatures thrive and grow, the earth is tended like a seed, and all both reap and sow. By all are labour's fruits enjoyed, and none goes hungry there; all gifts are prized, for all employed, and all have love to spare.

2. Each brother's paid his worth for toil, no sister may go poor; when one's in need, all rise to call compassion to their door; all flourish in that market-place where commerce wears a human face, true goods are bought and sold.

3. All seek the commonwealth of God, known or unknown by name; until that day we pledge our aid, and each as partner claim. Within the commonwealth of God all hearts weigh more than gold; since unending is the peoples find their home, and earth is clothed in heaven.

Within the commonwealth of God all creatures thrive and grow,
the earth is tended like a seed, and all both reap and sow;
by all are labour's fruits enjoyed, and none goes hungry there;
all gifts are prized, for all employed, and all have love to spare;

each brother's paid his worth for toil, no sister may go poor;
when one's in need, all rise to call compassion to their door;
all flourish in that marketplace where hearts weigh more than gold;
since commerce wears a human face, true goods are bought and sold.

All seek the commonwealth of God, known or unknown by name;
until that day we pledge our aid, and each as partner claim.
Within the commonwealth of God all peoples find their home,
unending is the peaceful road, and earth is clothed in heaven.

Words and Music: NINTH SEA BREEZE
© Doug Constable (after L.van Beethoven) 1995
Metre: 14 14 14 14

Acts 2.43-47a, 4.33-35
Christian Aid called for new hymns to mark its fiftieth anniversary, and this was my offering.
It took two years to find the music for this text: I was staying in SEA BREEZE Avenue, Singapore when I realized that the words wanted to sing along to the Ode to Joy in Beethoven's NINTH Symphony.

When you surveyed
Elegy for Philip

When you surveyed, with no note lost,
the place where Christ in glory died,
you sang forth pain and wonder crossed,
and heav'n poured love on earthly pride.

Like J.S.Bach's St Matthew Passion,
you began in low E minor,
resonant and sombre, warm; your
second line began to climb,
till, enharmonically, its closing syllable
set B flat major soaring upwards.
Subito then, D flat, veil-rending;
in that transfiguring chord
the Crucified
shook every hill's' foundations.
Now *pietà*: B natural minor,
to tonic-tomb, first womb-like home.

Your journey to that cadenced rest
tells forth a life of following Christ.
Wonder was in the promise confirmed:
abundant gifts received and shared.
As to contempt poured on your pride,
I never heard you boast,
save in the cross of Jesus your God.

Because of all you gave with love and thanks,
we're richly blessed with shafts of
love's enharmony:
this earth bound into heaven-on-earth in heavenly praise.

Eternally, what graces are to come?

What joys await us there!

100

Ym Methlem datguddiwyd y Gair a broffwydwyd	The prophesied Word was revealed in Bethlehem
ganrifoedd cyn 'ganwyd Mab Duw;	centuries before the Son of God was born,
ond nid yw Ef yno, trwy'r byd mae yn crwydro	but He is not there: He roves the wide world,
gan geisio rhoi'i law ar ein llyw;	looking to give us a guiding hand in life's journey.
can's tyfodd y Bachgen a gwelodd ein hangen,	For, as he grew up, the Boy saw our need,
anturiodd yn llawen ei ras,	and he held nothing back,
gan roi inni'r cyfan ohono ei hunan	but gave Himself to us wholly,
trwy weithio'n y Winllan fel Gwas.	working as a Servant in the Vineyard.
Dros gyd-ddyn bu'n brwydro, ond ca'dd ei dibrisio,	He battled on behalf of his fellow humans,
a'i ddedfryd oedd 'i hoelio ar groes,	was despised, condemned, nailed to the cross,
er iddo ledaenu ei gariad o'i deutu,	although his love knew no limits,
a'i fryd ar waredu 'mhob oes:	and he set out to free souls in every age.
rhoed Mab Duw, yr unplyg, 'r ôl dioddef y dirmyg,	The single-minded Son of God, after suffering scorn,
mewn bedd wedi'i fenthyg gan ddyn;	was given to a borrowed human grave;
ond nid yw Ef yno, gadawodd ei amdo	but He's not there: He stepped out of His shroud,
heb geisio cael clod iddo'i hun.	without seeking praise for Himself.
Daw atom yn dawel, fel mwsig yr awel,	He will come to us silently, like breeze-music,
yn gyson i ddiwel ei hedd;	steadily pouring out his peace.
trwy ddyfnder ei gariad derbyniwn wahoddiad	Through His deep love we receive a unique invitation
dihafal ein Ceidwad i'w wledd:	to our Saviour's feast.
boed inni ei ganfod a dod i'w adnabod	Let us look for and acknowledge him,
yn Gyfaill diddarfod drwy'n hoes,	as a faithful Friend for ever,
gan chwennych ei gwmni a dathlu ei eni	seeking His company
trwy foli Gorchfygwr y Groes.	by praising Him, the Victor of the Cross.

This lyric, by the late Alice Evans, won the prize at the National Eisteddfod 2010 for a new carol for the service of Plygain. The (paraphrasing) translation is mine.

'Plygain' traditionally refers to singing at cock-crow on Christmas morning. Most if not all Plygain carols have a marked emphasis on the connection between Incarnation and Atonement – between the birth in the stable and salvation won on the cross. This carol is no exception.

Nowadays services are held, mostly in the evening, sometime between Advent and Candlemas. Anyone may present themselves, singly or in a group, and, unaccompanied, sing their 'carol y Plygain'. I know of no other form of service so able to warm the heart.

Alice Evans (d.2017) © 2011 Doug Constable © 2011

TŶ GWYN MAWR 668 668 D

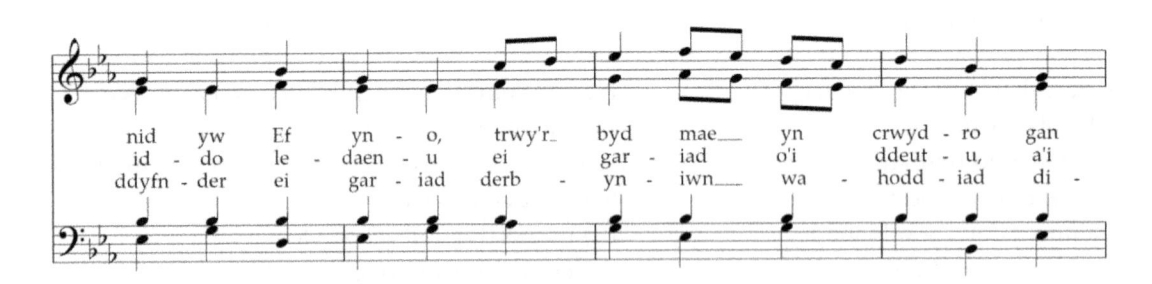

♩ = 104

1. Ym Methlem datguddiwyd y Gair a broffwydwyd gan-rifoedd cyn ganwyd Mab Duw; ond nid yw Ef yno, trwy'r byd mae yn crwydro gan geisio rhoi'i law ar ein llyw; can's

2. Dros gydddyn bu'n brwydro, ond cadd ei ddibrisio, a'i ddedfryd oedd 'ihoelio ar groes, er iddo ledaenu ei gariad o'i ddeutu, a'i fryd ar waredu 'mhob oes: rhoed

3. Daw atom yn dawel, fel miwsig yr awel, yn gyson i ddiwel ei hedd; trwy ddyfnder ei gariad derbyniwn wahoddiad dihafal ein Ceidwad i'w wledd: boed

tyfodd y Bachgen a gwelodd ein hangen, anturiodd yn llawen ei ras, gan roi inni cyfan ohonno ei hunan trwy weithio'n y Winllan fel Gwas.

Mab Duw, yr unplyg, 'rol dioddef y dirmyg, mewn bedd wedi'i fenthyg gan ddyn; ond nid yw Ef yno, gadawodd ei amdo heb geisio cael clod idd-o'i hun.

inni ei ganfod a dod i'w adnabod yn Gyfaill diddarfod drwy'n hoes, gan chwennych ei gwmni a dathlu ei eni trwy foli i Gorchfygwr y Groes.

101

MERCY 888 66

Words and Music
Doug Constable © 2001

♩ = 98

1. You break the bar, the yoke, the rod, upraise a people long down-trod; for humankind to life's new birth; Wise, ever faithful, you are God: Lord, show Yourself today! Lord, show Yourself today!

2. You cross from heaven's bright throne to earth, call Fool, You make the world Your hearth: Lord, show Yourself today!

3. You shine in darkness Your great light, dispower oppressors of their might; Strong Source of Love, for You fight: Lord, show Yourself today!

4. Disarm us all; defuse despair; douse flames of hate; make peace our prayer; turn guns to ploughshares ev'rywhere: Lord, show Yourself today!

5. Now may your will be wholly done by ev'ry friend of your dear Son, till all are saved, You are one: Lord, show Yourself today!

You break the bar, the yoke, the rod,
upraise a people long down-trod;
for ever faithful, you are God;
Lord, show yourself today!
Lord, show yourself today!

You cross from heaven's bright throne to earth,
call humankind to life's new birth;
Wise Fool, you make the world your hearth;
Lord, show yourself today!
Lord, show yourself today!

You shine in darkness your great light,
dis'power oppressors of their might;
strong Source of love, for love you fight;
Lord show yourself today!
Lord, show yourself today!

Disarm us all; defuse despair;
douse flames of hate; make peace our prayer:
turn guns to ploughshares everywhere;
Lord, show yourself today!
Lord, show yourself today!

Now may Your will be wholly done
by every friend of Your dear Son,
till all are saved, in You are one;
Lord, show yourself today!
Lord, show yourself today!

Isaiah 9.1-4; Micah 4.3-4; 1 Corinthians 1.18-25
This music was composed on the day we heard from Mercy ZYAMBO, a friend in Zambia, that her family was in desperate need.